D0467621

101

QUESTIONS ABOUT

SLEEP AND DREAMS

THAT KEPT YOU AWAKE NIGHTS . . . UNTIL NOW

. . . . .

FAITH HICKMAN BRYNIE

. . . . .

TFCB TWENTY-FIRST CENTURY BOOKS
MINNEAPOLIS

Twenty-First Century Books
A division of Lerner Publishing Group
241 First Avenue North
Minneapolis, Minnesota 55401 U.S.A.

Website address: www.lernerbooks.com

Illustrations courtesy of Laura Westlund

Cover photograph reproduced with permission from Images.com/CORBIS

Photographs reproduced with permission from: © Victoria & Albert Museum, London/Art Resource, N.Y.: p. 8; © James Holmes/Photo Researchers, Inc.: p. 13 (all); © Steven M. Platek, M.D.: p. 30 (both); AP/Wide World Photos: pp. 36, 100; © Mary Beth Angelo/Photo Researchers, Inc.: p. 37; © Eye of Science/Photo Researchers, Inc.: p. 47; © Don Cravens/Time Life Pictures/Getty Images: p. 53; © Reuters/CORBIS: p. 57; © Dr. T. J. Beveridge & S. S. Schultze/Visuals Unlimited: p. 75; © Gerard Lacz/Animals Animals-Earth Scenes: p. 90; © Oscar Burriel/Photo Researchers, Inc.: p. 94; © Bettmann/CORBIS: p. 96; © Anthony Bannister, Gallo Images/CORBIS: p. 121; © CC Studio/Photo Researchers, Inc.: p. 126; © Culver Pictures, Inc./SuperStock: p. 137; "It's a Dog Life" © 1997 by Joe M. Giannandrea http://www.geocities.com/itsadogslifeyukon: p. 148

Library of Congress Cataloging-in-Publication Data

Brynie, Faith Hickman, 1946-
101 questions about sleep and dreams that kept you awake nights . . . until now /
by Faith Hickman Brynie.
   p. cm.
Includes bibliographical references and index.
ISBN-13: 978-0-7613-2312-9 (lib. bdg. : alk. paper)
ISBN-10: 0-7613-2312-0 (lib. bdg. : alk. paper)
1. Sleep—Miscellanea.   2. Dreams—Miscellanea.   3. Sleep disorders—Miscellanea.
I. Title: One hundred one questions about sleep and dreams that kept you awake nights . . . until now.   II. Title.

QP425.B79 2006   612.8'21—dc22   2005017276

Manufactured in the United States of America
1 2 3 4 5 6 – JR – 11 10 09 08 07 06

CONTENTS

ACKNOWLEDGMENTS

The author appreciates the contributions of all those who helped make this book a reality. Much gratitude is due to those teachers whose students provided some of the most thought-provoking questions answered here: Rob Schrembeck and Sarah Costic, Brunswick High School, Brunswick, Ohio; Diane Buhler, Cardinal Mooney High School, Sarasota, Florida; Kay Collins and Mollie Marot, Badin High School, Hamilton, Ohio; Kimberly Williams, Miller Place High School, Miller Place, New York; Mark Stephansky, Whitman-Hanson Regional High School, Whitman, Massachusetts; Christina Stubblefield, Faith Fellowship Christian School, Evans Mills, New York; and Chris Imperial, Albany State University, Albany, New York.

The author also wishes to thank the following experts for their insightful critical reviews: Stephen Sheldon, director, Sleep Medicine Center, Northwestern University Medical School, Chicago, Illinois; Marcos Frank, University of Pennsylvania School of Medicine, Department of Neuroscience, Philadelphia, Pennsylvania; Eric H. Chudler, Department of Anesthesiology, University of Washington,

Seattle, Washington; Jack Davis, a physician in private practice in Kalispell, Montana; and Patrick J. Burns, neurologist and sleep specialist, and Tim Hoselton, assistant manager, of the Sleep Medicine Center in Kalispell, Montana. Thanks also to Joel Benington, Department of Biology, St. Bonaventure University, St. Bonaventure, New York, for his assistance with adenosine research; and to Steve R. Wills, who authored the feature on sleep clinics in chapter 4.

The greatest of all gifts is given by those who support day by day a process that is its own reason for being. Thank you, Ann, for being more than a mother could ever dream of. Thank you, Lloyd, for being you. Sleeping or waking, you are my center and my sustenance.

FOREWORD

I wander all night in my vision,
Stepping with light feet, swiftly
and noiselessly, stepping and stopping,
Bending with open eyes over the shut eyes of sleepers .
• WALT WHITMAN •

In "The Sleepers," poet Walt Whitman observes sleepers in their beds, and he sees that they are all the same. Old or young, male or female, the moneymaker, the prisoner, the unrequited lover: they all sleep. "I dream in my dream all the dreams of the other dreamers, and I become the other dreamers," Whitman writes.

We all sleep, and in our sleep, we are all more or less the same. We spend about one-third of our lives with our eyes closed, our muscles relaxed—quiet and unresponsive—becoming aware of what goes on around us only in extreme circumstances. Sleep is an irresistible force in our lives, and in recent years we have learned a lot about it. We know that each time we sleep, the patterns of electrical activity in our brains change from the rapid waves of wakefulness to the slow waves of deep slumber. Then, periods of intense brain activity begin, much like those experienced during wakefulness. But the sleeper still sleeps, with eyes moving rapidly beneath closed lids and . . . perhaps . . .

dreaming the vivid dreams of REM sleep. In our dream world, we may see ourselves at home or in foreign lands, interacting with friends or strangers. In our dreams, we may perform the tasks of daily life, walking to school or taking out the trash. Sometimes we do the impossible: we fly high above the earth on invisible wings, hobnob with celebrities, or reunite with loved ones long lost.

Sometimes, our dreams turn against us, and as Whitman imagined his way into the twilight world of all sleepers, he saw there, too, the demons of the night. Perhaps all sleepers see them as Francisco de Goya did in his 1799 etching *The Sleep of Reason Produces Monsters*.

"The Sleep of Reason Produces Monsters" by Francisco de Goya (1799)

Or perhaps we personalize their form, seeing inside ourselves those fears we dare not express or acknowledge when awake. But whatever the dream, sleep is, above all else, a loss of reason. The common sense of waking life shuts down. Although most dreams are mundane, the ones that fascinate us most lead us into realms of fantasy. We go, as sleep expert William Dement put it, "quietly and safely insane" each night. Miraculously, whether we dream long and large or not at all, our sleep time refreshes and restores. Sleepers awaken stronger, smarter, and healthier from a slumber they can, ironically, neither control nor comprehend.

This book attempts to answer only 101 of the thousands of questions that keep curious sleepers and sleep scientists awake nights. In these pages, you'll get an idea of what happens in a typical night's sleep and how human sleep changes from infancy to old age. You'll look briefly at whether all animals sleep—and if they do, how. Questions and answers in this book probe the mysteries of how body and brain maintain a twenty-four-hour cycle and how losing sleep negatively affects health, both mental and physical. This book also includes some questions and answers about common sleep disorders and explores what little we know—or guess—about the puzzle of dreams and dreaming. As you read, you'll discover how much and how little we know about sleep. You'll share in the excitement of those sleep scientists who are exploring a "new frontier" as unknown as the expanses of the universe. "Now I pierce the darkness," Whitman wrote in his poem. That's what this book tries to do.

CHAPTER ONE

QUESTIONS

ABOUT HOW AND WHY WE SLEEP

Sleep is not some biological luxury.
Sleep is essential for basic survival.

• RONALD E. DAHL •

What is sleep? Sleep is hard to define, but you know it when you see it. The sleeper is either sitting or lying down, moving little if at all, with eyes closed. The sleeper's awareness of the environment is reduced. Soft sounds and gentle touches elicit no response, although loud noises and forceful contact will. In comparison with wakefulness, sleep appears to be a state of inactivity, with both body and brain at rest.

But appearances can be deceiving, and scientists aren't satisfied with what they see on the outside. They look inside the body to define sleep. In sleep laboratories, instruments measure breathing frequency and effort, airflow, oxygen levels in the blood, pulse rate, heart rate, and more. Sensors detect the strength and frequency of eye movements and the tension inside muscles. Most important, a device called an electroencephalograph records changes in electrical activity in the brain. The tracing the machine makes is an electroencephalogram, or EEG. Its intricate patterns of peaks and valleys reveal changes in the impulses traveling among nerve cells.

EEGs show that the brain functions differently when sleeping and awake. When a person is awake and active, the EEG shows mostly waves of the "beta" type. Beta waves are rapid waves. They cycle between thirteen and thirty-five times every second. At such times, eye movements and muscle tone vary, depending on what the person is doing.

In the minutes before sleep, however—when eyes close and the body relaxes—eye movements and muscle tone diminish, and the number of beta waves decreases. "Alpha" waves, which cycle eight to twelve times per second, take their place. Slow, rolling eye movements begin, and the sleeper loses awareness of what's going on in the environment. At that time, it seems that sleep has begun, although the sleeper can be easily aroused to insist, "I wasn't asleep." Surer signs of sleep are distinctive peaks called "sleep spindles" that appear later in the EEG.

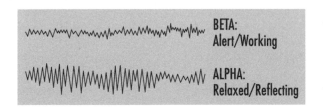

BETA:
Alert/Working

ALPHA:
Relaxed/Reflecting

These are EEG tracings of beta and alpha "brain waves." The electrical activity of nerve cells in the brain produces these patterns.

Is all sleep the same?

No. Human sleep occurs in a sequence of five stages that repeat several times during an average night's sleep. The stages show up on an EEG as shifts in the amplitude (height) and frequency (number of waves per second) of brain waves.

Stage 1: As the sleeper drifts into slumber, the EEG shows a series of fast, low-amplitude signals. Eyelids slowly open and close and the eyes move, but the body's big muscles relax. The slightest disturbance can arouse the sleeper, who may also experience a sensation of falling accompanied by sudden muscle contractions, something like the involuntary "jump" response to being startled.

Stage 2: Brain waves grow slower, settling into a rhythm of "theta" waves. These are waves of medium amplitude that cycle four to eight times per second. Eye movements stop. The sleeper is still easily awakened, although less so than in stage 1. At this stage, the EEG shows occasional bursts of activity called "sleep spindles. They last only a second or two, and they may have something to

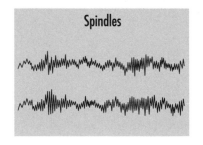

Spindles

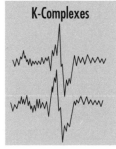

K-Complexes

Spindles are short bursts of electrical activity in the brain that last only a second or two. A spindle can be part of a K complex.

do with blocking out anything that might arouse the sleeper. Also at this stage, "K complexes" appear in the EEG. They are sharp, negative, high-voltage waves, followed by a slower, positive component. Sometimes, spindles are part of K complexes. About half of an adult's total sleep time is spent in stage 2 sleep.

Stage 3: Large, slow "delta" rhythms show up on the EEG, interspersed with smaller, faster waves. The sleeper is difficult to wake now. Deep sleep has begun.

Stage 4: The delta waves take over almost entirely in this stage. These high-amplitude waves are slow; they cycle fewer than four

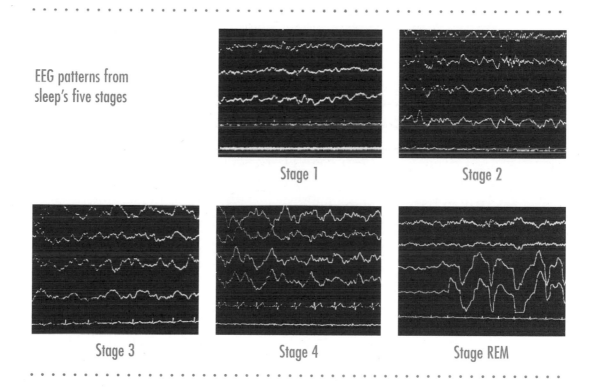

EEG patterns from sleep's five stages

Stage 1

Stage 2

Stage 3

Stage 4

Stage REM

times in a second. This is the deepest of all the sleep stages. If awakened during this stage, the sleeper feels groggy and disoriented. Bed-wetting, sleepwalking, and sleeptalking occur most often during stage 4 sleep. Together, stages 3 and 4 are called slow-wave sleep. During slow-wave sleep, the brain's use of fuel (glucose from food) declines by about 20 percent.

REM sleep: The fifth stage is so different from the other sleep stages that it gets a name of its own. It is REM sleep, and it makes up about 20 to 25 percent of a good night's sleep for an adult. REM stands for "rapid eye movement." Watch someone sleeping, and you'll have no trouble seeing when REM sleep begins. The eyes dart and jerk actively beneath closed lids, stop for a while, and then start moving again. Breathing becomes rapid, irregular, and shallow.

Inside the body, heart rate increases and blood pressure rises. Major muscles keep their tone, but they do not move. The body is almost completely paralyzed. The only muscles that continue to work are the heart, diaphragm (breathing), eyes, and the smooth muscles of the blood vessels and internal organs.

During REM sleep, the EEG records low-amplitude beta waves like those of wakefulness. In this stage, the brain's use of glucose for fuel rises to levels equal to—or even greater than—those measured during waking hours. This heightened level of brain activity gives REM its other name—paradoxical (meaning "a seeming contradiction") sleep. Although dreams can happen during any stage, REM sleep is prime time for dreaming.

Typically, a night's sleep begins with between seventy and ninety minutes of sleep stages 1 through 4, moving progressively from one to the next. Then comes a brief REM period of about ten minutes. This cycle

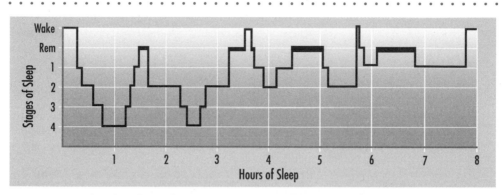

During a typical night's sleep, sleep stages 3 and 4 disappear, while REM periods lengthen.

repeats from three to six times during the night, with REM periods growing longer in each cycle. Stages 3 and 4 occur early in the night. They disappear from the cycle as morning approaches, and stages 1 and 2 predominate, sometimes interrupted by a brief period of wakefulness.

Many factors can affect this average cycle. Athletes, for example, spend more time in slow-wave sleep (stages 3 and 4) than the less physically fit do. Growth hormones are released during slow-wave sleep, and growing children and teens spend a larger portion of their sleep in those stages than older people do.

Sleep history can change the pattern. A person who has lost sleep one night may, on the next night, move quickly through the first stages of sleep and enter REM sooner than normal—as if in a hurry to make up for some of the REM sleep that was lost.

The environment can affect the sleep cycle, too. During REM sleep, the body's ability to regulate body temperature falters, so hot weather or cold rooms can interfere with REM sleep.

"We don't know why we need to sleep," says Robert McCarley, a sleep expert at Harvard University. University of Chicago sleep researcher Alan Rechtschaffen agrees. He calls the mystery of why we sleep "a huge hole in biological knowledge." Still, there's no shortage of theories about why humans, like most other mammals, spend a lot of time sleeping:

+ **Survival advantage**: Sleep may get an animal "out of harm's way" at certain times. For example, prey species that are active at night avoid predators that hunt in daylight. (The counterargument is that sleep is a disadvantage to survival. While they sleep, animals cannot care for their young, find food, or defend themselves against attackers.)

+ **Energy saving**: Sleep may conserve energy. On average, animals burn calories at a slower rate during sleep than when they are awake and active.

+ **Energy replenishing**: During sleep, body cells or nerve cells may restock depleted energy reserves.

+ **Housecleaning**: During sleep, the brain may "take out the trash," getting rid of unimportant information and clearing space for processing new inputs the next day.

+ **Making memories**: During sleep, the brain may move newly learned information or experience into more permanent memory storage. (For more on this idea, see chapter 3.)

One thing seems clear, however. Sleep is not, as was once thought, a time for restoration of the body. It's the brain that needs sleep. Other organs of the body repair themselves as well during "resting wakefulness" as when we sleep. The cerebral cortex—the brain's thin outer layer, which processes thoughts, learning, and purposeful action—does not. The frontal lobe of the cortex, which lies behind the forehead, is the brain's most active region during the waking hours. It handles reasoning and decision making when we are awake, but it nearly shuts down during slow-wave sleep. This may mean that sleep

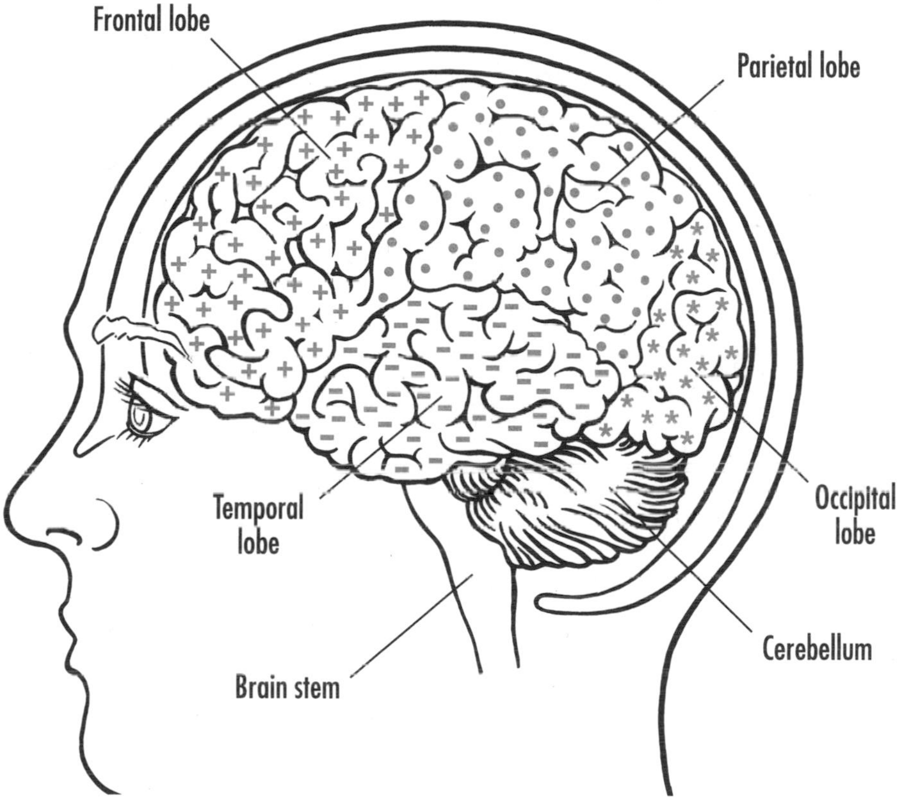

Frontal lobe

Parietal lobe

Temporal lobe

Occipital lobe

Cerebellum

Brain stem

The cortex is the brain's thin outer layer. The frontal lobe, behind the forehead, is its center for reasoning and judgment.

gives the nerve cells there a chance to repair themselves. Without sleep, they may become so low on energy or so poisoned by waste materials that they cannot function efficiently.

Even a single night without sleep impairs performance on tests of comprehension, concentration, creativity, and problem solving—all frontal-lobe functions. It makes sense, then, that if lack of sleep impedes the performance of this region, sleep must be doing something to maintain it. Sleep studies provide some evidence that this is true. Researchers find that the longer you go without sleep, the more slow-wave sleep (stages 3 and 4) you get when next you nod off. This suggests that non-REM sleep may help the brain recover from the efforts it makes—or the damage it incurs—during waking hours.

REM sleep may have a different function and operate in a different way—perhaps involving neurotransmitters—from other sleep stages. Neurotransmitters are molecules that transmit impulses from one nerve cell to another. Three important ones are norepinephrine, serotonin, and histamine. They latch onto receptors on the surfaces of nerve cells, like keys fitting into locks. When they do, some induce a nerve impulse to begin; others prevent a nerve impulse from moving on. During REM sleep, the release of these neurotransmitters slows or ceases. This "time-out" may be important, sleep expert Jerome Siegel suggests, because the receptors stimulated by these neurotransmitters get desensitized during the waking hours. Allowing the receptors to "rest" and regain their sensitivity may be essential to the normal functioning of nerve cells.

Sleep scientist William Dement has another idea. He thinks that sleep—especially REM sleep—acts as a workout for the brain. It develops "mental muscles." The self-stimulation of dreaming trains the brain, Dement says, to respond to real-world challenges. It organizes communication pathways among neurons. Since new brain cells

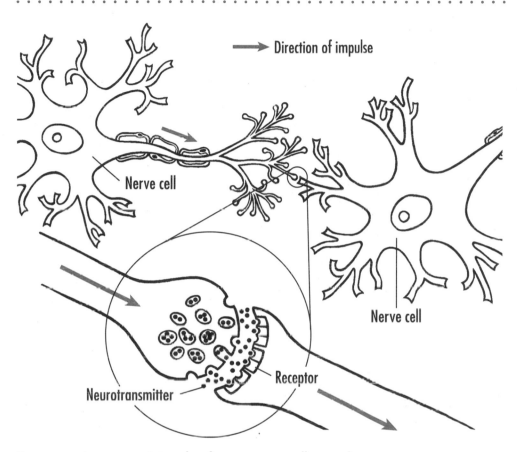

Direction of impulse

Nerve cell

Nerve cell

Neurotransmitter

Receptor

Neurotransmitters transmit impulses from one nerve cell to another.

are formed throughout life, Dement thinks adults may "need REM sleep to integrate new brain cells and to shape the connections made by existing ones."

Another possible function for sleep may be regulation of the emotions. Who hasn't gone to bed at night angry or sad only to wake feeling more accommodating, positive, and in tune? Says Milton Kramer of New York University, "It's as if an emotional thermostat kicks in during the night to warm the mood that may have chilled during the day."

Why do I sleep more when I'm sick?

When you are fighting an infection, your brain triggers your sleep centers. You feel a strong, sometimes overpowering, need to sleep. Some of the proteins that come from the cell walls of bacteria and viruses promote sleep, as do the proteins the immune system makes as weapons against them. For example, cytokines are immune proteins that attach to the membranes of some body cells and not others. They carry messages between cells and enhance their ability to withstand the attack of disease-causing microbes. Some cytokines, such as interleukin-2, promote sleep generally. Others, such as interferon-a, promote slow-wave, non-REM sleep.

While you sleep, your pituitary gland sends out commands to step up production of the white blood cells that fight invading microorganisms. CD4 cells in the blood, also called helper T cells, trigger the production of antibodies. Antibodies are proteins that lock onto invading microbes and mark them for destruction. More of them are made and dispersed during sleep than during the waking hours. CD8 cells, also called killer T cells, destroy invading microbes by splitting their cell membranes with enzymes. They also destroy body cells infected with viruses. Canadian researchers studied the numbers of CD4 and CD8 immune cells in the blood of "good sleeper" and "poor sleeper" volunteers. People in both groups were healthy, but good sleepers had higher levels of CD4 and CD8 cells in their blood than the poor sleepers did.

Is sleep needed for growth?

In children and young adults, the brain releases relatively large amounts of growth hormone during sleep—especially during slow-wave sleep, stages 3 and 4. The hormone stimulates cells to produce proteins that build new cells and enlarge existing ones. The production of new cells surges late at night and in the early morning hours. People who are deficient in growth hormone sleep less and in briefer, interrupted periods. Whether the deficiency causes sleep problems or the sleep problems cause the deficiency is unknown.

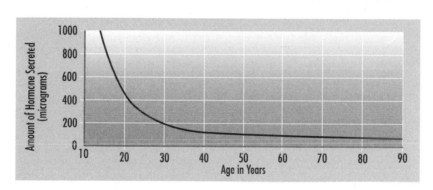

Adapted from "Sleep Quality and Endocrine Markers of Sleep Quality," by Eve Van Cauter for the John D. and Catherine T. MacArthur Foundation Research Network on Socioeconomic Status and Health.

Our nighttime secretion of growth hormone is greatest when we are young.

How does sleep change from birth to age twenty?

The types and amounts of sleep change during the first two decades of life. Healthy, full-term newborns spend two-thirds of their lives sleeping—while their tired parents lose between 400 and 750 hours in baby's first year! The immature brains of the very young do not produce the characteristic EEG patterns of the sleep stages seen in children and adults. Instead, "active sleep" and "quiet sleep" are observed and measured in fetuses and newborns.

During active sleep, limbs move and the fetus or newborn breathes erratically. Eye muscles move, and breathing may pause briefly. Although active sleep differs from REM sleep in important ways (such as the EEG pattern it produces), it will eventually develop into the REM sleep of the older child and adult.

During quiet sleep, the fetus or newborn lies immobile, making only occasional jerking movements. Breathing is regular and eye movements are rare. Quiet sleep develops into the non-REM sleep stages 3 and 4 that first appear between three and six months after birth. Unlike children and adults, newborns begin their sleep periods with active sleep before they move into quiet sleep.

About one month after birth, infants begin to consolidate their sleep into a long nighttime period and shorter daytime periods. Until about six months, active and quiet sleep are divided approximately equally.

AGE	"QUIET SLEEP"	"ACTIVE SLEEP"	REM	Non-REM
Fetus/Newborn	P	P	A	A
Infant	C	C	A	A
Child/Adult	A	A	P	P

P = present, A = absent, C = changing

At one year of age, children sleep approximately fifteen hours daily. The need declines to twelve hours daily by age four. Children of this age fall rapidly into stage 4, deep sleep, making them difficult to wake. They may blink, move their hands, make noises during sleep, and skip the first REM period that adults usually experience about seventy to ninety minutes into their sleep period. One or two daytime naps are the norm among preschool children, although individual needs and habits vary.

Between ages five and seven, children develop the same REM/non-REM patterns as adults. After they start school, they begin to sleep less on weekdays and more on weekends and vacations. Total sleep time declines from 11 hours at age five to about 9.25 hours at age twelve. Somewhere between 20 and 41 percent of elementary school children experience significant sleep difficulties. Nightmares, night terrors, and sleepwalking sometimes develop in this age group, as can "bedtime resistance."

Unmet sleep needs appear by the sixth grade. Many sixth graders go to bed late, take longer to get to sleep, and sleep less than they should. Sixth graders complain of drowsiness in the morning, signaling the arrival of the delayed sleep phase syndrome typical of adolescence (see "Cheer Up, Sleepy Teens," page 59). At this time, behavioral and social problems may be a sign of sleep deprivation.

Sleep changes dramatically in the teen years. Time spent in slow-wave sleep (stages 3 and 4) decreases and becomes a smaller percentage of total sleep time. REM sleep time remains constant, but it shrinks as a percentage of total sleep time.

Adolescents feel sleepier during the day and wake more frequently at night than do younger people, perhaps because of both shifting hormones and social demands. The highest level of sleep disturbances occurs between ages fifteen and seventeen. People in that

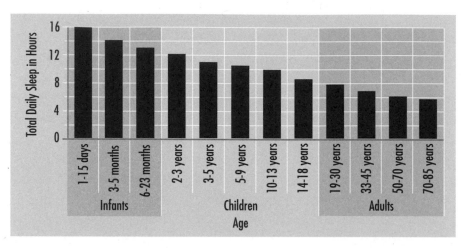

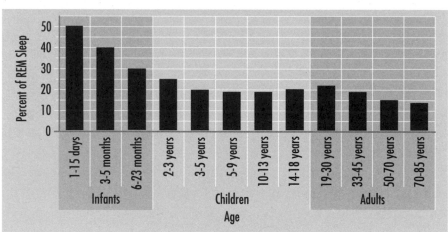

Graphs courtesy of Eric Chudler, University of Washington. Data from H. P. Roffwarg, J. N. Muzio, and W. C. Dement. "Ontogenetic Development of the Human Sleep-Dream Cycle." *Science*, Volume 162 (1966), 604–618.

Total sleep time and the percent of sleep time in the REM stage change with age.

age group take longer to get to sleep, wake more during the night, and move more in their sleep than do younger or older teens.

Why do babies sleep so much? No one knows, but some experts think sleep may play important roles in brain development. As development progresses, connections among neurons form and reform, taking on new and better configurations—something like remodeling a house. Working with kittens, Marcos Frank and his team at the University of California, San Francisco, studied development of the brain's visual processing centers. The researchers masked one of the kittens' eyes for six hours, partially blocking the animal's vision. Then some of the kittens were allowed to sleep for six hours, while others stayed awake. The kittens that slept developed twice as many "remodeled" connections among neurons in their brains compared with the animals that stayed awake with the eye mask removed. They even developed more connections than did awake animals that continued to have one eye covered. The amount of development depended not on REM sleep, but on the deep, slow-wave sleep of stages 3 and 4.

Frank says there are two possible explanations for his findings. Maybe the nerve impulses that were transmitted during the experience are "replayed" and reinforced during slow-wave sleep. Or perhaps growth hormones that promote the formation of connections between neurons are released then. Either way, this is the first direct evidence that sleep modifies neuronal connections in the developing brain.

Do elderly people need less sleep than younger people do? The elderly sleep lightly. As we age, we get less slow-wave sleep and less REM sleep. The number, density, and duration of sleep spindles and K complexes decline in older people. The elderly wake more frequently than younger adults do, although they fall back to sleep equally well. Senior citizens report more drowsiness and fatigue during the day, more and longer naps, and earlier bedtimes than younger adults do. They have more difficulty falling asleep and staying asleep than younger people do. Getting up to urinate, pain from diseases such as arthritis, and side effects of medications are among the reasons.

On average, elderly people get less sleep than they did when they were young, although whether they *need* less is debated. Some experts

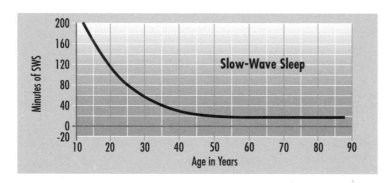

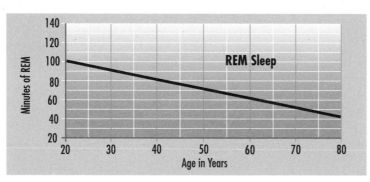

Adapted from "Sleep Quality and Endocrine Markers of Sleep Quality," by Eve Van Cauter for the John D. and Catherine T. MacArthur Foundation Research Network on Socioeconomic Status and Health.

As we age, our slow-wave and REM sleep times diminish.

say that older people don't need as much sleep; they perform better mentally after sleep deprivation than young people do. Other experts disagree, suggesting that elderly people may simply have more ways to compensate for the effects of sleep loss.

Does losing sleep make you age faster?

Maybe. A research team at the University of Chicago let eleven healthy young men sleep only four hours a night for six nights. Then the scientists measured how well the men's bodies handled the basic food source, glucose. (Starches and sugars in food break down into glucose. Glucose sugar in the blood is the body's main energy source.) After the sleepy men ate breakfast, the level of glucose in their blood rose higher than it should have and took longer to return to normal. Their bodies made adequate amounts of the hormone insulin, which stimulates cells to take up glucose and use it for energy, but their cells did not respond to insulin as vigorously as they normally would. (That's the same pattern physicians see in people who develop type II diabetes.) The levels of stress hormones in their blood were higher than normal, and their thyroid glands were less active. Because their blood profiles resembled those of much older people, the researchers concluded that missing sleep might contribute to age-related diseases such as high blood pressure and loss of mental acuity.

Is a coma the same as sleep?

The two states look a lot alike to an observer. In both, awareness of the environment is lost. Muscles relax, sensitivity to pain diminishes (although weakly in natural sleep), and memory is lost. But the sleeper can be awakened by sound, light, or touch whereas the comatose person cannot. In EEGs, still other important differences show up. People who are in a coma do not produce the complex, active brain-wave patterns seen in normal sleep. Instead, their brain waves are slow, weak, and synchronized, showing few or no K complexes and sleep spindles. Alpha and beta waves may appear, but they may be continuous and widespread throughout the brain. The pupils of the eyes are permanently constricted and do not respond to light.

Comas usually result from brain injury and seldom last for long. The exception is the "vegetative state" described as "wakefulness without awareness." Such patients regain their sleep-wake cycle, and may be aroused by pain or other stimuli, but they show no clear signs of perceiving, understanding, acting, or communicating. Nevertheless, EEGs show that some components of sleep survive, even in people who are deeply comatose, and the return of normal sleep patterns can coincide with a return to normal consciousness.

Does sleepiness cause yawning?

Open the mouth wide, stretch the muscles of the jaw and upper body, take a slow breath in, and then exhale quickly. What have you done? You have yawned. Many animals, including humans, yawn. They do it involuntarily. The signal that initiates a yawn comes from a particular brain region, the paraventricular nucleus (PVN) of the hypothalamus. It stimulates other brain cells in both the brain stem and the hippocampus to produce the muscle contractions we call a yawn. The PVN also makes chemical messengers that may induce yawning. Its production of one called adrenocorticotropic hormone (ACTH) increases dramatically during sleep and just before waking.

To figure out why we yawn, Italian researchers videotaped the spontaneous yawns of premature infants in intensive care units. The babies were good subjects for studying yawning because they had little opportunity to imitate the yawning of others and their brains were still maturing. The infants yawned before sleep, but they also yawned as they awoke. The researchers concluded that yawning signals a changing state of arousal or alertness. That may explain why athletes often yawn before competition.

Despite what you may have heard, yawning has nothing to do with increasing the body's oxygen supply. In experiments, subjects yawn just as much in oxygen-rich air as they do in an oxygen-poor atmosphere. Yawning is, however, a response to boredom. When researchers showed students ages seventeen to nineteen music videos and color bar test patterns, those who saw the test patterns yawned nearly twice as often as those who watched videos, and their yawns lasted longer.

Is yawning contagious?

"Yawning is extraordinarily contagious," says Robert Provine, the pioneer of yawning research. "Seeing a person yawn triggers yawns. Reading about yawning causes yawns. Sitting in a room thinking about yawning triggers yawning," he says. Some experts think this happens because yawning evolved as a means of communication. It may help animals, including humans, coordinate their behavioral responses to changing conditions in the environment.

That may explain why some people are more susceptible to contagious yawning than others. Psychologist Steven Platek and his team at Drexel University in Philadelphia gave sixty-five college students per-

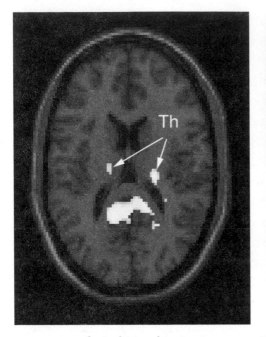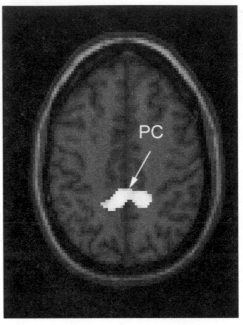

Brain scans of people "catching" a "contagious" yawn show significant activity (the light areas) in two regions: the thalamus (Th) and the posterior cingulate (PC). These brain areas process personal memories and basic emotions.

sonality tests. The tests measured their empathy, or how well they perceived and responded to the mental states of other people. Platek then observed through a one-way mirror (so his subjects didn't know they were being watched) how the students responded as they watched videos of people yawning. The students who scored high for empathy yawned more often in response to the videos than their less compassionate peers. This suggests that yawning is a form of social communication.

Does it matter
what position
I sleep in?

For infants, the answer is yes. Sleeping on the back reduces the risk of sudden infant death syndrome (SIDS). For the rest of us, the answer is "probably not," although sleeping on your back may make you more prone to snoring, and stomach-down sleeping invites indigestion. Sleep position may, however, reveal something about your daytime behavior, according to British sleep expert Chris Idzikowski. He surveyed one thousand people, looking for links between their resting posture and their personality. He defined some common sleep positions and gave names and personality assessments to people who assume them. You can decide for yourself whether you agree with his conclusions:

+ Fetal position: This is the most common of all sleeping positions, with 41 percent of Idzikowski's subjects saying they assume it. It's twice as common among women as men. It's a sign of a person who's tough on the outside but has a sensitive heart, Idzikowski says.

+ "The Log" (15 percent): Easygoing, sociable people who like being part of the crowd.

+ "The Yearner" (13 percent): Suspicious, cynical, stubborn, slow to make a decision.

+ "The Soldier" (8 percent): Quiet, demanding of self and others.

+ "The Freefall" (7 percent): Talkative, brash, sensitive to criticism.

+ "The Starfish" (5 percent): Good friends and good listeners who shy away from attention to themselves.

Fetal, 41%

Log, 15%

Yearner, 13%

Soldier, 8%

Freefaller, 7%

Starfish, 5%

Does the position you sleep in reveal something about your personality? You decide.

How often do I move during sleep?

Individuals vary, moving as few as ten to as many as eighty times in an eight-hour period. The average range is thirty to fifty times.

Is it possible to sleep with one or both eyes open?

No one goes to sleep or remains asleep with open eyes, although sleepwalkers and children who have night terrors open their eyes.

But the champions at eyes-open sleeping are not humans. They're ducks. Niels Rattenborg, a sleep researcher at Indiana State University, filmed mallards sleeping as they often do—in neat rows. The birds at the ends of the row sleep with their outermost eye open. The mallards in the middle either sleep with both eyes closed or show no preference for which stays open. Rattenborg thinks the ducks on the ends keep an "eye out" for predators, while those inside the row enjoy the protection their sentinels give them. Periodically, the ducks change position, giving each a turn at guard duty.

While sleeping with one eye open, the opposite side of the mallard's brain is awake, but its activity is somewhat less than during waking time. The side of the brain opposite the closed eye sleeps. The more threatened the ducks feel, the more likely they are to sleep with one eye open; and the open eye is always in the direction of the perceived threat. The birds sleep this way only when the risk of predation is high. They resume sleeping with both eyes closed when predators aren't around. Ducks aren't the only animals that sleep one-half of the brain at a time. Penguins and cockatiels do it, too. So do some marine mammals.

Hibernation looks like sleep, but it isn't. Animals such as the black bear that hibernate with body temperatures above 77°F (25°C) sleep normally during hibernation, but those whose body temperatures sink lower lose the brain-wave patterns characteristic of sleep. Hibernation protects animals from the cold by slowing their body functions, lowering their body temperature, and decreasing their need for food. In hibernating

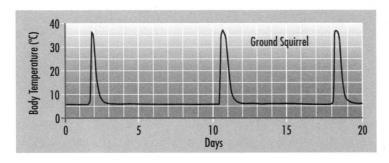

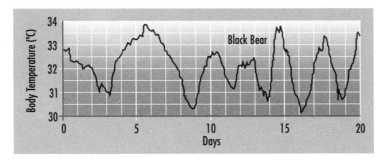

Adapted from Norman F. Ruby. "Hibernation: When Good Clocks Go Cold." *Journal of Biological Rhythms* (August 2003), 276.

Ground squirrels hibernate at near-freezing temperatures. Black bears stay much warmer — and rouse more often.

ground squirrels, for example, the heart rate drops from its usual two hundred to three hundred beats per minute to between three and ten. Blood oxygen level drops to 2 percent of normal, and body temperature goes from 98.6°F (37°C), the same as humans', to a mere 36° to 41°F (2° to 5°C). Obviously, no human could survive such declines, even during sleep.

Hibernating animals warm to their normal body temperature and rouse from hibernation at regular intervals. At such times, they are active for several hours. They eat, drink, check for intruders, or even give birth—as female bears do. Their immune systems also "jumpstart" at those times, acting against disease-causing microbes that may have lain dormant during the low temperatures of hibernation.

Following active periods, they enter periods of non-REM, slow-wave sleep. On the EEG, these sleep periods resemble the recovery sleep that non-hibernating animals get after a period of sleep deprivation. Scientists aren't sure, however, that hibernating animals need to wake up to sleep. If they are kept awake after coming out of hibernation, they accumulate no more "sleep debt" than they normally would.

Slumbering Sea Lions and Other Enigmas

· · · · ·

Oh sleep! It is a gentle thing, beloved from pole to pole.

SAMUEL TAYLOR COLERIDGE

· · · · ·

Do all animals sleep? The answer depends on how you define sleep. All placental mammals and birds sleep by the human-style definition. They have alternating periods of REM and non-REM sleep. However, the sleep habits of different species vary greatly. Sea lions sleep

A colony of sea lions sleep on top of each other on a pier in San Francisco.

six hours daily, while giraffes sleep only three and bats sleep twenty. Sleep-cycle times vary, too. A mouse's cycle lasts nine minutes. Elephants' take as long as two hours. Birds have REM sleep periods that last only five to six seconds.

The question gets harder to answer when scientists study the most primitive mammals, the monotremes. Monotremes have hair and nurse their young from mammary glands as placental mammals do, but they lay eggs. Only three species of monotremes live today. One is endangered and not available for study, but the other two have "slept for science."

One, the duck-billed platypus of Tasmania and Australia, has non-REM sleep and what appears to be REM sleep. The animal's eyes move beneath closed eyelids, and its muscles twitch. In fact, for all outward appearances, the platypus is a champion REM sleeper, spending seven to eight hours at day in REM, an amount greater than any other animal's. Appearances can be deceiving, however, and some experts question whether the platypus has true REM sleep. In placental mammals and

Elephants stand during non-REM sleep but lie down for REM sleep.

birds, the brain stem initiates REM sleep and then the forebrain gets into the act, generating EEG readings that look a lot like those of the waking brain. In the platypus, there is no forebrain action during REM sleep. The action is confined to the brain stem, just as it is in another monotreme, the short-beaked echidna, or spiny anteater. It shows no outward signs of REM sleep. Its eyes do not move and its muscles do not twitch. Its brain shows a mixture of REM and non-REM waves.

Scientists who wonder how sleep evolved think these differences are important. Placental and monotreme mammals evolved from a common ancestor, but about 130 million years ago, their paths separated. So did the evolution of sleep, with REM and non-REM becoming distinctively different sleep states over time. It's possible that the modern echidna is like the primitive mammalian or even reptilian ancestor of modern birds and mammals. A clear distinction between REM and non-REM sleep may have evolved gradually from the mixed REM/non-REM pattern of a primitive ancestor like the echidna.

Birds sleep, but their sleep patterns differ from those of mammals, and vary with season and circumstance. White crown sparrows, for example, don't stop to rest during their 2,672-mile (4,300-km) migrations between Southern California and Alaska. They may fly as far as 300 miles (500 km) at night and feed all day. They don't sleep while flying or take "power naps" to make up for their sleep loss. How do they stay awake for such long periods? No one knows.

As we survey the remainder of the animal kingdom, the picture gets increasingly complicated. Reptiles appear to sleep, but their brain waves do not show REM/non-REM patterns. Fish and amphibians go into resting states that resemble sleep, but too few species have been studied in enough detail to decide whether their low-activity periods qualify as sleep. Among animals without backbones, sleeplike states—in which the body is in repose, arousal is difficult, and muscle activity and rates of breathing and circulation slow—are seen in squids, octopuses, and "sea hair" mollusks. Crayfish have slow-wave electrical activity in their brains that compares with sleep in mammals.

Some research suggests that even insects may sleep. In about the seventh hour of their rest phase, bees enter their deepest sleep phase, when their breathing is slowest. They don't have REM sleep, but they have periods when they move their antennae rapidly. One characteristic of sleep is that the need for it increases the longer the animal stays active. That increase has been seen in cockroaches and scorpions, which seem to get "recovery sleep" just as people do.

Ralph Greenspan and Paul Shaw, researchers at the Neurosciences Institute in San Diego, studied sleep in fruit flies. They hooked vials containing tiny fruit flies to a machine that emits an inaudible sound wave. Any movement of a fly disrupted the sound wave and sent a signal to a computer, giving the scientists an accurate record of the insects' activity patterns.

They found that fruit flies, like people, sleep at night and sometimes nap in the early afternoon. Also like people, soft sounds won't wake the flies, but loud sounds will. Fruit flies get sleepy when given antihistamines, the active substance in many "drowsy-formula" cold and allergy remedies. When they got caffeine in their food, they had trouble sleeping—just as coffee-guzzling humans do. Like human infants, young flies needed the most sleep. The scientists tapped the vials, keeping the flies awake for long periods. The longer the flies went without sleep, the harder it became to keep them awake.

Sleeping may not be much different among animals, but waking is. In reptiles and other cold-blooded animals, the sensory and motor areas of the brain stem wake the animal. In warm-blooded animals, higher brain regions—the neocortex in mammals and the neostriate in birds—sound the wake-up call. Despite these differences, it's a myth that smarter animals sleep longer or have more REM sleep, says University of California, Los Angeles, sleep scientist Jerome Siegel. The "dream sleep" times of humans and other primates, arguably the most intelligent animals, are neither high nor low. In fact, highly intelligent whales and dolphins have little REM sleep. Instead, they fit what Siegel calls "the general rule of maturity at birth." The less well-developed the nervous system of the young, the more REM sleep is needed, perhaps for the maturation of nerve cells and the formation of communicating pathways between them.

CHAPTER TWO

17 QUESTIONS

ABOUT WHEN AND
HOW MUCH WE SLEEP

Life is something you do when you can't get to sleep.
• FRAN LEBOWITZ •

I don't do mornings. Am I weird?

We all know both types: the "larks," or "morning people," who wake happily with the sunrise, eager to meet the day; and the "owls," or "night people," who hit their stride when the sun goes down and who can't seem to wake up before noon. The preference for morning and evening is not imagined and is probably only partly learned. A lot depends on the genes inherited from parents. (Genes are pieces of DNA in the nucleus of cells. DNA is the master molecule that controls what goes on in living cells. It makes living things different from each other.) One of the genes that controls waking and sleeping in humans is called *Clock.*

ARE YOU A LARK OR AN OWL?

Decide whether you mostly agree or mostly disagree with each of these statements:

1. Bedtime for me is usually 10 P.M. or earlier.
2. I'd love to get up at 9 A.M. or even later if I could.
3. I usually feel sleepy before 10 P.M.
4. If I didn't use an alarm clock, I probably wouldn't get up until lunchtime.
5. Getting up in the morning is easy for me.
6. I feel lousy when I first get up.
7. I feel hungry soon after I get up.
8. I don't want to exercise in the morning, and if I am forced to, I do poorly.
9. I would rather take a difficult test in the morning than at any other time of day.
10. If I get to bed after midnight, I feel fine the next day.
11. Even if I get to bed late, I wake up around my usual time.
12. If I could choose my own school or work hours, I would prefer to start in the afternoon and work until midnight.
13. I feel my best before noon.
14. I would rather stay up late to study or do homework than get up early.
15. If I could do as I please, I would usually get up before 9 A.M.

Score yourself. For every *odd*-numbered item that you *agree* with, give yourself one point. For every *even*-numbered item that you *disagree* with, give yourself one point. If you score 11 to 15, you are definitely a lark, or morning person. Five or less makes you an owl, or evening type. A score of 6 to 10 means you are a "mixed" type, with both morning and evening preferences.

Researchers think differences in the *Clock* gene may explain—at least in part—why some people bounce out of bed full of energy whereas others drag until afternoon.

How much sleep do I need?

Probably more than you are getting. Before the electric lightbulb became a fixture in every home, the average adult slept about nine hours a night. Today, the average is closer to seven. One in every four Americans says he or she isn't getting enough sleep to feel alert during the day. Two in five say that daytime sleepiness interferes with their activities at least a few days a month. These are symptoms of too little sleep. This chronic "sleep debt" results from the way we live. Writes *Sleep Thieves* author Stanley Coren, "When the pressure of work, alarm clocks, social schedules, and advanced technology is removed, people tend to sleep longer." Research suggests many of us could benefit from more sack

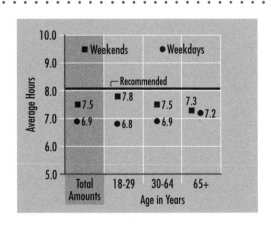

Modified from 2000 Omnibus Sleep in America Poll, National Sleep Foundation.

The average adult in the United States gets too little sleep on weekdays and attempts to make up for sleep loss on weekends.

time. Scientists at Stanford University in California let fifteen healthy college students sleep longer than they usually did. The students reported better moods and performed better on tests requiring quick action.

Can I make up for lost sleep?

Getting too little sleep creates a "sleep debt." That is, losing sleep one day means sleeping longer the next—and feeling an increased need to do so. The body demands that about one-third to one-half of total lost sleep be recovered hour for hour. (For example, if you lose three hours of necessary sleep one night, you'll sleep an extra one to one and one-half hours the next—if you don't set an alarm.) The slow-wave stages 3 and 4 are made up first. Then REM. There is little recovery of stage 2 sleep, but the ability to recover from sleep loss seems total. Healthy adults can make up lost sleep with no apparent long-term ill effects.

How does missing sleep affect the body?

The physical effects of sleep loss include increased appetite, a drop in body temperature, increased sensitivity to pain, and feelings of drowsiness. The immune system, which fights off disease, is slower and weaker to attack invading microbes. Shakiness, visual problems, and headaches go along with sleep loss. When scientists test sleep-deprived volunteers, they find that physical abilities decline less than do mental skills. For example, army researchers found that soldiers can shoot a fixed target as well after ninety hours of sleep deprivation as when well rested. But if targets pop up at random, performance drops. The ability to handle two tasks at the same time declines, even after only a few hours' sleep loss. In one experiment, college students who missed a night's sleep could balance their bodies and perform a difficult computer task as well as they had before. But when asked to do both at once, both balance and computer skills failed.

How does missing sleep affect the mind?

Say the letters of the alphabet. It's easy, right? Count from one to twenty-six. That's easy, too. Now try saying numbers and letters alternately by ones (A1, B2, C3 . . .), twos (A1, C3, F5 . . .), or threes (A1, D4, G7 . . .). These tasks require sustained attention. It's hard, but you can do it. Now try doing it after you have missed a night's sleep. That's what sleep scientists Mary Carskadon and William Dement asked of six healthy young volunteers who stayed awake not one night, but two. During that time, the volunteers complained of bad moods and feeling sleepy.

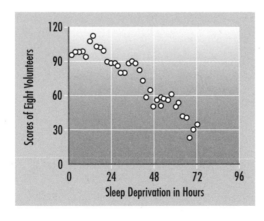

Adapted from G. Belenky. "Sleep, Sleep Deprivation, and Human Performance in Continuous Operations," Walter Reed Army Institute of Research.

This graph shows performance on an addition-subtraction test during seventy-two hours without sleep. The score is the product of speed and accuracy.

Their skill in simple arithmetic declined, as did their ability to perform the letter-number task. Also, the time they needed to fall to sleep fell steadily. By 6:00 A.M. after their first night of sleep loss, they fell asleep in less than a minute. (The normal time for falling asleep is ten to twenty minutes.) The subjects needed not one but two nights of recovery sleep to get their performance scores back to where they were before the experiment.

In another ingenious experiment, researchers at the City University of New York gave students a math test. The computer allowed the students to choose problems at five levels of difficulty while taking the test. When students had lost sleep the night before, they got as many problems right as when they were well rested, but they chose easier problems. Furthermore, they didn't realize they were expending less effort.

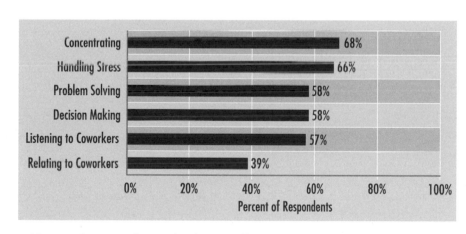

Solving problems and getting along with others is difficult for people who feel sleepy at work or at school.

Sleep loss affects more than mental performance. It affects emotions. In one survey, two-thirds of respondents said they have trouble concentrating and handling stress at work when they are sleepy. Other effects include irritability, impatience, poor concentration, apathy, hostility, and loss of control over emotions. Writes physician Ronald Dahl, "If faced with a frustrating task, a sleep-deprived teenager is more likely to become angry or aggressive. Yet, in response to something humorous, the same subject might act more silly or inane. [This suggests] a decrease in inhibition or conscious control over emotions following sleep loss."

How does sleep loss affect the brain?

University of California, San Diego, researcher Sean Drummond takes "pictures" inside living brains at work. In one experiment, he asked people to memorize lists of words. After normal sleep, the task activated areas of the brain's left prefrontal cortex. (Located behind the forehead, this is one of the areas most active during the waking hours.) After sleep deprivation, scores on the word test fell by half, but activity in the prefrontal cortex increased. Furthermore, regions not normally used went to work. It seemed that the brain recruited new regions to help get the job done. "Without this compensation, folks would do much worse than they do," Drummond says.

Can missing sleep make me sick?

Even a brief sleep loss affects the numbers and kinds of disease-fighting cells and chemicals the immune system makes. For example, if you stay up until 3 A.M. for just one night, the next day you'll have 30 percent fewer of the

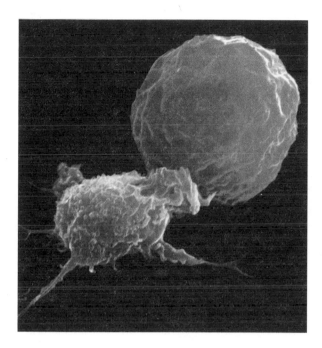

The natural killer cell on the left is attacking the cancer cell on the right. If you lose sleep, you produce fewer natural killer cells.

virus fighters called natural killer cells. That may make you more vulnerable to colds and flu.

Alexandros Vgontzas, at Pennsylvania State University, restricted sleep in healthy young volunteers by only two hours a week. The mildly sleep-deprived individuals showed marked changes in their immune systems. The amount of interleukin-6 in their blood increased 40 to 60 percent. Tumor necrosis factor, or TNF, showed a 20 to 30 percent increase. Both are inflammatory substances that the body normally makes in response to an injury. They increase the risk of chronic diseases such as high blood pressure, heart disease, and diabetes.

Sleep also influences how well your body responds to immunizations. University of Chicago researchers examined the effects of sleep deprivation on healthy young men who received flu shots. The scientists measured the numbers of disease-fighting antibodies the men developed in their blood. Ten days after getting their shots, the men who got the vaccine after six nights of sleep deprivation (four hours a night) had developed fewer than half as many antibodies as the men who had slept seven and one-half hours or more—even though they were allowed plenty of recovery sleep after they got their immunizations. In another study, volunteers slept or stayed up for one night after getting vaccines to prevent hepatitis A. After four weeks, those who went to bed on time had nearly twice as many anti-hepatitis antibodies in their blood as those who missed a night's sleep.

How can I know if I am getting enough sleep?

Healthy young people should be able to perform well throughout the day without feeling sleepy. If you nod off when you sit quietly and try to read or listen, you probably aren't getting enough sleep at night. If your reactions are sluggish and you find your attention wandering, even briefly, you may be sleep deprived.

It's not just the total amount of sleep that matters. Sleep must be continuous. Disruptions reduce sleep's ability to restore and refresh. The more frequently you awaken, the greater the effect.

Why do some people need more sleep than others do?

Although the average adult needs about eight hours of sleep nightly, some people routinely sleep a lot more or a lot less. Natural "long sleepers" and "short sleepers" vary in more ways than how much they sleep. Long sleepers (who regularly sleep nine hours or more at night) need more REM sleep than the average person does, and they spend most of their extra sleep time in that stage. Although the absolute amount of slow-wave sleep (stages 3 and 4) is the same for long and short sleepers, it's a greater percentage of a short sleeper's total sleep time.

At night, long sleepers secrete more of the "drowsiness hormone" melatonin, and its level stays higher in their blood longer. Their body temperature hits its lowest point later in the early-morning hours. The level of the arousal hormone cortisol in their blood peaks later in the morning, too.

Researchers at the University of Pittsburgh studied twelve short sleepers, who regularly sleep less than six hours a night. Their work

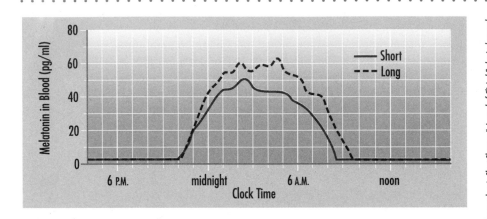

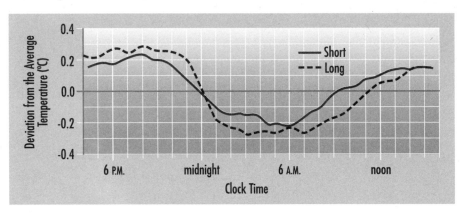

Adapted from D. Aeschbach et al. "A longer Biological Night in Long Sleepers than in Short Sleepers." *Journal of Clinical Endocrinology and Metabolism* (January 2003), 26–30.

Long sleepers have higher nighttime levels of the "sleep hormone" melatonin than do short sleepers. They also have lower body temperatures.

and exercise habits were no different from those of longer sleepers, but they were more irritable, talkative, and easily distracted than longer sleepers. They had an inflated sense of self-importance and were more likely to take risks. Other studies suggest that short sleepers are more neurotic and less creative than long sleepers. They are also more anxious and worry more.

Short sleepers may not actually need less sleep. They may simply handle sleep deprivation better. They experience the same changes in temperature and hormone levels in the evening as do longer sleepers, but they "resist" them longer. They are less responsive to the chemical and nerve cell triggers that induce sleep, and they may be better at the self-stimulating, self-arousal brain activities that promote alertness during the waking hours.

WHO SLEEPS BADLY?

Researchers in Sweden interviewed more than eighteen thousand people over a twenty-year period. Those most likely to report disturbed sleep were

- Female,
- Older than forty-nine,
- Ill, and/or
- Working at hectic, physically strenuous, or shift-work jobs.

Those reporting fatigue were most often

- Female,
- Younger than forty-nine,
- Relatively wealthy,
- Ill, and/or
- Working hectic or physically strenuous jobs or putting in a lot of overtime.

Can I train myself to sleep less?

Some people say they have trained themselves to sleep less, but researchers challenge that notion. David Dinges and his team at the University of Pennsylvania tested people who averaged four, six, or eight hours of sleep a night. Those who slept less than eight had slower reaction times and impaired memory. Their problem-solving skills matched those of people who didn't sleep at all for two nights. Dinges's colleague Hans Van Dongen says that sleep restriction seriously impairs the functions of the human nervous system "even if we feel we have adapted to it." Stanford psychiatrist Christian Guilleminault says that individuals vary greatly in their response to sleep deprivation, but "everyone becomes impaired by sleep deprivation, and . . . abnormal responses will be triggered in some people."

How long can a person go without sleep?

No one knows for sure, but some competitors in rocking chair competitions are said to have stayed awake for as long as nineteen days. However, the best-known and best-studied record was set in 1965, when Randy Gardner, a seventeen-year-old high school student from San Diego, stayed awake for 264 hours and 12 minutes (about eleven days). He used cold showers, loud music, and endless games of pinball to stave off sleep. He suffered many ill effects. After one night's lost sleep, he had trouble focusing his eyes. After two nights, he grew moody and irritable, and he had difficulty with speech. His memory failed him on the fourth day, and he started seeing things that weren't there. He also imagined himself to be a famous football player. Near the end of his ordeal, he stopped speaking.

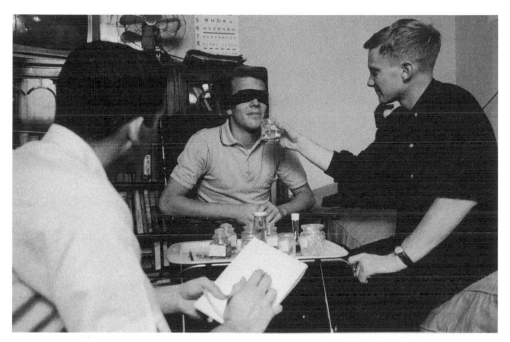

During his sleep deprivation experiment, Randy Gardner tries to identify scents offered to him by another student.

As amazing as Gardner's story is, even more amazing is the recuperative power of sleep. When at last he hit the sack, Gardner slept for nearly fifteen hours. In a few days, he was his old self again, showing no apparent long-term ill effects.

Missing sleep makes me hungry. Is that normal?

Leptin is a hormone secreted by fat cells. It is one of the body's messengers that control appetite. It sends to the brain the message, "I'm full. I don't want any more." Sleep-deprived people have a lower level of leptin in their blood than those who are well rested. They say they feel hungry after losing sleep—not for salads and fresh fruits, but for fatty, sugary, and starchy foods.

No one knows why sleep loss leads to increased appetite. It's possible that the brain signals the body to increase food intake in order to raise lowered body temperature or to provide the increased energy more hours of awake time require. Or maybe it's psychological. Sleep loss makes us feel tired and bored. We don't feel like doing much else, so we eat more.

Will losing sleep make me gain weight?

Many researchers say yes. In fact, sleep loss may be partially responsible for the epidemic of obesity that is sweeping the United States, especially among young adults.

Texas researchers studied nearly four hundred subjects ages eleven to sixteen. Those who were obese slept less than those of normal weight. For each hour of sleep loss, the risk of obesity rose 80 percent. Disturbed sleep was related to diminished physical activity. For every hour spent awake during the night, physical activity during the day declined by 3 percent, which could contribute to gaining weight.

Studying more than eight thousand children, Japanese researchers found a strong relationship between late bedtime, short sleeping hours, and obesity. Scientists in Spain found that people who sleep nine or more hours a day were significantly less likely to be obese than those sleeping six hours or less. The researchers found that the risk of obesity increased by 30 percent for every hour of television watching. They also found that the risk of obesity decreased by 24 percent for every hour of sleeping.

Although historical records show that we've grown heavier as our hours of sleep have decreased, experts caution that they can't be sure about the cause-and-effect relationship. Are we overweight because we sleep less, or do we sleep less because we are overweight? Or is some other factor, like stress or the electric light, promoting both overweight and sleep loss?

Until these questions are answered, it makes sense to include a good night's sleep in any plan for weight control. Does that mean long hours in bed? Probably not. Robert Vorona and his team at Eastern Virginia Medical School in Norfolk studied over one thousand people. Their conclusion? An extra twenty minutes of sleep per night was associated with a lower, healthier body weight.

Does noise affect sleep?

Yes, and probably more than we realize. REM sleep and slow-wave sleep time decrease with continuous, nightly sound levels around 45 decibels. That's about the loudness of a humming refrigerator. At that same level and higher, sleepers report sleeping poorly and awakening more frequently. Increases in stage 2 (lighter sleep) along with decreases in REM sleep occur at about 60 decibels. That's the loudness of a normal conversation.

Does losing sleep affect job performance?

Yes, and the effects are large. Approximately half of all American workers report that sleepiness interferes with their job productivity. The cost of sleepiness-related accidents in the workplace runs about $16 billion in the United States and $80 billion worldwide.

One in five working adults admits making errors either occasionally or frequently because of sleepiness. In some vocations, mistakes on the job can be life-threatening. For example, one study found that sleep-deprived medical interns detected fewer irregular heart rhythms in their patients than did well-rested interns. Compared with well-rested surgical residents, those deprived of sleep made more errors and were slower to perform certain delicate surgical tasks. The researchers concluded that patient care may be compromised if "a fatigued, sleep-deprived doctor is allowed to operate, administer an anesthetic, manage a medical crisis, or deal with an unusual or cognitively demanding clinical case."

Another risky occupation is air traffic control. Federal Aviation Administration researchers gave "fatigue tests" to air traffic controllers who worked eight- and ten-hour shifts. The controllers did well on the tests for four days, but on the fifth day—especially after working a rotating night shift—their performance declined. They reported feeling tired, sleeping less, and having more "bad moods" by the end of their workweek. Among other workers in the transportation industry, "sleepiness surpasses alcohol and drugs as the greatest identifiable and preventable cause of accidents in all modes of transport."

Søren Kierkegaard may have been thinking about napping when he wrote, "Sleeping is the highest accomplishment of genius." Brahms napped at the piano while he composed his famous lullaby. Napoleon napped between battles. Churchill maintained that he had to nap in order to cope with his wartime responsibilities. Geniuses such as Edison and Leonardo da

New England Patriots' quarterback Tom Brady is famous for taking naps before big games. He stretched out for forty-five minutes on the locker-room floor before Super Bowl XXXIX in January 2005. Later, he led his team to their third NFL Championship.

Vinci napped. According to sleep expert William Dement, "Nature definitely intended that adults should nap in the middle of the day." The human brain, it seems, is programmed to fall asleep not only at night but also for a brief period in midafternoon. A post-lunch siesta for as little as fifteen to thirty minutes can dispel bad moods and restore flagging concentration.

Napping is common among people who report daily "information overload." It can also help people do non-desk jobs better. In one study, long-haul truck drivers were tested on driving simulators. They were allowed five hours of sleep at night. They then "drove" the simulators for twelve hours. For half their "trips," the drivers lay in darkness between 2 and 5 P.M. For the other half, they read or watched TV during that time. After their afternoon breaks, they continued "driving" until eight o'clock the next morning. At the simulators, they received rewards for faster completions. They were penalized for crashes, accidents, and exceeding the speed limit. Those who napped crashed less often and reached their destinations sooner than the non-nappers. The truckers who napped said they felt less sleepy. More important, their reaction times were faster, and they performed skilled driving maneuvers more reliably.

Nap researchers at Harvard University's Vision Science Laboratory trained college students in a visual task, locating lines on a computer screen. The volunteers trained and tested for four times a day: 9 A.M., noon, 4 P.M., and 7 P.M. During the first session, the students got better at the task, but they showed no further improvements after the noon testing. In the afternoon and evening sessions, their performance got worse. But napping around 2 P.M. made a big difference. A thirty-minute nap stopped the decline in the students' scores. An hour-long siesta raised their evening performance to equal the best morning level.

Why was the longer nap more effective? Recordings of brain waves showed more than four times as much slow-wave and REM sleep in the longer naps compared with the shorter ones. Slow-wave sleep, the researchers think, serves as an "antidote to burnout." "You work on something until your brain screams, 'No more, no more!'" says sleep researcher Robert Stickgold. "Then you take a little nap and you're all better."

Cheer Up, Sleepy Teens

· · · · ·

*Sleep is being put on the back burner in teenagers,
and that affects mood, cognitive functioning,
the choices they make, and their quality of life.*

LAUREN BROCH, DIRECTOR
SLEEP-WAKE DISORDERS CENTER
NEW YORK PRESBYTERIAN HOSPITAL

· · · · ·

Observe the behavior of the common species *Teenagerus americanus*. This fascinating life-form stays up half the night watching TV, playing computer games, talking on the telephone, or listening to music before eventually tumbling into bed somewhere around midnight. When the alarm jangles the next morning, the creature stumbles half-blind from bed to shower, mumbling unintelligibly—a habit of speech that persists through mid-morning.

Yawning, nodding off, and daydreaming persist throughout daytime hours, dominating especially the after-lunch periods. Representatives of the species appear energetic in late-afternoon sports, jobs, and social activities, but nod off doing homework. *Teenagerus americanus* becomes most active around 9 or 10 P.M., often after everyone else in the family has gone to bed. Then the cycle starts again—except on weekends, when nearly half of the species sleeps past 9 A.M. and one in ten sleeps past noon.

If *Teenagerus americanus* sounds a lot like you or someone you know, it's no surprise. Researchers Amy Wolfson at Holy Cross University and Mary Carskadon at Brown University surveyed more than three thousand high school students in Rhode Island. Between ages thirteen and nineteen, the students went to bed later and decreased their total sleep time by nearly an hour. They slept less because they went to bed later. Those who stayed up late and slept late on weekends reported more daytime sleepiness, blue moods, and problems falling asleep and staying asleep. "Most of the adolescents surveyed do not get enough sleep, and their sleep loss interferes with daytime functioning," Wolfson and Carskadon concluded.

What may surprise you is how much sleep teens actually need. On the average, if allowed to sleep as long as they like and wake naturally, most teens will sleep 8.5 to 9.25 hours each night. Even when sleep is adequate, those who keep an irregular schedule report more daytime sleepiness than those who get up and go to bed at the same time every day. Those who sleep on a regular schedule also feel more alert and are more sleep efficient (that is, they spend more of their time in bed actually sleeping).

Perhaps because of the many

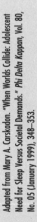

Adapted from Mary A. Carskadon. "When Worlds Collide: Adolescent Need for Sleep Versus Societal Demands." *Phi Delta Kappan*, Vol. 80, No. 05 (January 1999), 348–353.

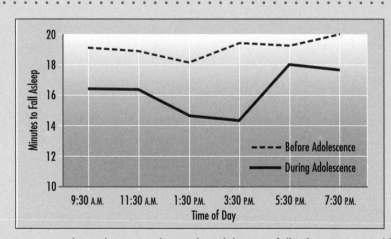

Even when given a ten-hour sleep period at night, adolescents fall asleep more quickly during the day than do younger people.

changes that are occurring in their bodies as they grow and mature sexually, adolescents actually need more sleep than eleven-year-old children do. However, many teens find it hard to feel sleepy before 11 P.M. or even later. For reasons no one understands, adolescents experience a "teenage phase shift." Their brains don't produce enough melatonin, one of the chemicals that cause drowsiness. Without it, they stay up too late and get too little sleep. Even when they get enough sleep at night, teens may feel drowsy during the day, especially in the early afternoon. Between 1:30 and 3:30 P.M., they fall asleep quickly and easily.

Carskadon says sleepy teens live under a "kind of gray cloud." They grow accustomed to feeling tired and sleepy, and "forget what it's like to feel good, and how much more efficiently you can do things." Fatigue interferes with learning at school. Tired students have trouble paying attention. And, because sleep is important for forming and maintaining memories, they forget what they try to learn. "The students may be in school, but their brains are at home on their pillows," Carskadon says.

Relationships suffer, too. Tired teens feel angry, sad, and stressed. "It's crystal clear that kids who sleep less report more depressed mood," she says.

There are two good ways to cheer up sleepy teens. One is to "grow out of it." German researchers found that the tendency to stay up late and sleep late in the morning disappears abruptly around age twenty. Until then, the best solution is to get more sleep. To improve your chances of doing just that, keep a sleep diary for a week or two. Record when you go to bed, when you wake up, and whether you had difficulty falling asleep or staying asleep. Write down how you felt when you rose, the times when you felt sleepy during the day, and when you napped intentionally. If you find you are getting too little sleep, you can take the following steps to help yourself:

- Examine your commitments. If you have taken on too many responsibilities at school or work, cut back to a more manageable load.
- Plan a daily schedule that allows you to spend at least nine hours in

bed. Plan to go to bed and get up at the same time every day.

- Stick with your schedule. If you must stay up late, make it no more than two hours past your usual bedtime, then take an afternoon nap the next day.
- Don't nap too late in the day or you will have trouble getting to sleep at night. Many people find that early afternoon is the best naptime.
- Get some exercise every day, but avoid anything more strenuous than a relaxing stroll in the evening.
- Establish a quiet time in the evening before bedtime. Turn off the computer, TV, radio, and CD player, and take only emergency telephone calls. Take a warm bath and enjoy a glass of milk or a cup of herbal tea. Read something light and pleasant and settle into a comfortable position before sleep.
- Turn off mobile phones and text messaging services. Interruptions erode sleep quality, and they can cause daytime sleepiness as great as losing several hours of sleep can.
- Keep lights dim in the evening. Turn them on bright in the morning.
- Regulate the temperature in the bedroom. Being too hot or too cold can interfere with sleep.
- Cut out coffee and caffeinated sodas after noon. Avoid tobacco and alcohol; they disrupt sleep.
- Never drive when you're tired!

CHAPTER THREE

22 QUESTIONS

ABOUT SLEEP
AND THE BRAIN

*We sleep, but the loom of life never stops, and the
pattern which was weaving when the sun went down
is weaving when it comes up in the morning.*

• HENRY WARD BEECHER •

**What happens
in the brain
during sleep?**

The brain needs sleep, but it never shuts down.
In fact, some nerve cells in the brain fire five to
ten times more often during certain sleep stages
than they do during wakefulness. During sleep,
the brain stem, located at the base of the brain
where it meets the spinal cord, maintains basic life functions, including
heartbeat and breathing. The thalamus, which acts as the brain's dis-
patching center for incoming information from the senses, filters out
what's not important (traffic noise, wind blowing) and lets in what is
(smoke detector, baby crying). Overall, brain activity diminishes during
slow-wave sleep, but it increases during dreaming.

Patterns of heightened activity and relative rest vary with the stages of sleep. During non-REM sleep, most neurons in the brain stem oscillate between relative quiet and intense activity. The neurons of the cerebral cortex and higher brain regions reduce their activity slightly. These neurons do not work independently, however, as they do during

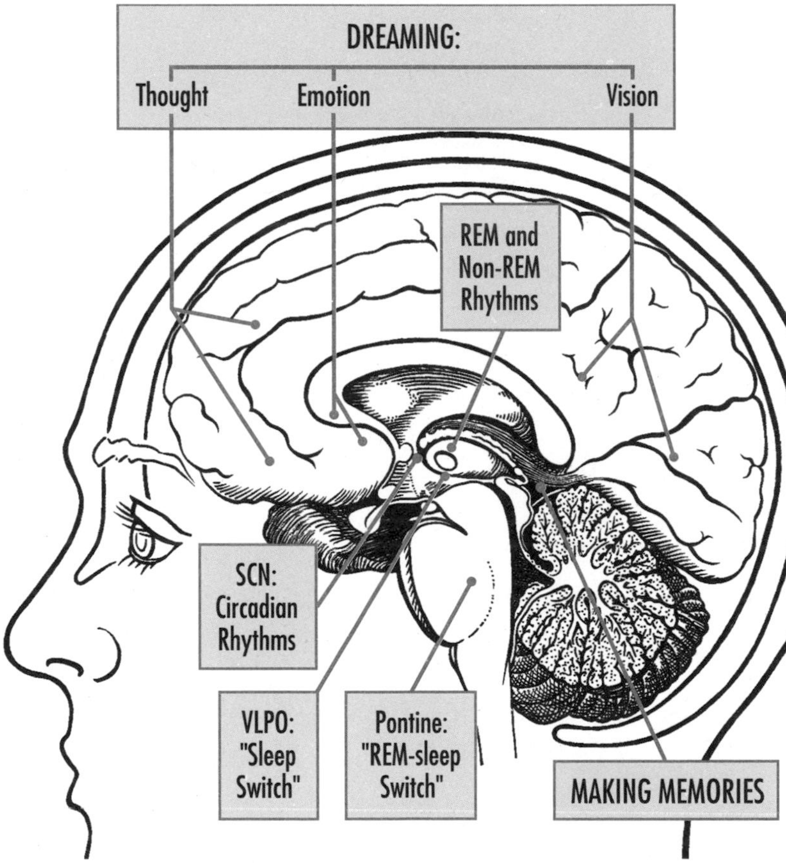

DREAMING:

Thought Emotion Vision

REM and Non-REM Rhythms

SCN: Circadian Rhythms

VLPO: "Sleep Switch"

Pontine: "REM-sleep Switch"

MAKING MEMORIES

Adapted from E. F. Pace-Schott and J. A. Hobson. "The Neurobiology of Sleep: Genetics, Cellular Physiology and Subcortical Networks." *Nature Reviews/Neuroscience* (August 2002), 592.

Many areas of the brain initiate, maintain, and regulate sleep.

the waking hours. They pulse more or less in synchrony, producing the characteristic EEG wave patterns of sleep stages 1 through 4. Noticeably active at this time are the cells of the ventrolateral preoptic nucleus (VLPO). This is the brain's main "sleep center." It plays a big part in initiating and maintaining sleep.

During REM sleep, the brain uses as much energy as it does during waking. Nerve cells in the brain stem are active, as are cells in the brain's centers for visual processing and emotion. They operate independently, as they do during the waking hours. They signal other nerve cells as rapidly—or even more rapidly—as during the waking hours. A group of cells localized in the pontine area of the brain stem is especially active during REM sleep, and it seems to act as the "REM switch."

What does the brain do during different stages of sleep?

Each stage of sleep has its own pattern of electrical activity and its own chemistry. Nerve cells in the brain make and release neurotransmitters. Neurotransmitters are molecules—proteins, amino acids, sometimes even gases. They leave one nerve cell and diffuse across a microscopic space. Then, on the surface of another nerve cell, they attach to a receptor site, like a key sliding into a lock. Once attached, they can cause the receiving nerve cell to fire. Or they can prevent, or inhibit, it from firing. What happens depends on the neurotransmitter and the nature of the receiving neuron.

Levels of neurotransmitters rise and fall in different brain regions as the sleeper moves through the sleep stages. For example, certain nerve cells in the thalamus, the brain's central relay station for directing impulses to other brain centers, release the neurotransmitter gas nitric oxide (NO). NO is released at a much lower rate during slow-wave sleep than during REM sleep or wakefulness. That fact suggests that NO may play an important role in regulating the activity of the thalamus. Its action may control how responsive the person is to what's going on in the environment.

Another neurotransmitter, acetylcholine, mainly activates neurons in the "thinking" centers of the brain's frontal cortex. It is released in large amounts at two times: during waking and during REM sleep.

Why do I go to sleep? "Sleep is not a passive thing," says University of Montreal neuroscientist Roger Godbout. "It is actively induced. There are parts of the brain that are responsible for keeping us awake, and another part of the brain that's responsible for keeping us asleep." One brain center known to trigger sleep is the VLPO (ventrolateral preoptic nucleus). This grape-size cluster of cells lies in the front of the hypothalamus. (The hypothalamus is a region in the underside of the brain, behind the eyes.) The VLPO acts as a "slumber switch," says Clifford Saper, a neurologist at Harvard Medical School. "The VLPO turns out the lights in the brain and lets it go to sleep."

Like all neurons, the nerve cells of the VLPO do their job chemically. One of the most important inhibitory neurotransmitters is gamma-aminobutyric acid (GABA). The nerve cells of the VLPO release GABA. Molecules of GABA bind to neurons in another part of the hypothalamus, the tuberomammillary nucleus (TMN). When it is active, the neurotransmitter histamine in the TMN promotes wakefulness. GABA from the VLPO shuts that system down. Without signals from the TMN saying "stay awake," sleep begins. The VLPO has no GABA receptors, so the inhibitory neurotransmitter doesn't affect it.

What keeps me asleep?

The VLPO stays active during sleep, keeping wakefulness at bay. Scientists have studied activity in the VLPO by measuring the amount of a protein called *fos* in its cells. Large amounts of *fos* are found in the VLPO only during sleep, when its cells are most active. Mice that lack the gene for making *fos* take twice as long to go to sleep and sleep 30 percent less than normal mice. The gene doesn't switch on and start *fos* production until after sleep begins, says Harvard's Robert McCarley. "Therefore, it can't trigger sleep, but it might be responsible for the continuity of sleep."

Why do I wake up?

The brain's main "stay awake" centers are located in the hypothalamus and the brain stem. A complex cocktail of neurotransmitters regulates them. The neurotransmitters include acetylcholine, norepinephrine, serotonin, and histamine. Some scientists think another neurotransmitter, hypocretin (also called orexin), is the main chemical that pushes the "awake button" in the hypothalamus. Brain cells that produce hypocretin are normally active during waking and inactive during sleep. "Naturally, we would always be asleep, but orexin floods the brain, waking us up," says University of California, Los Angeles, sleep scientist Jerome Siegel. Another "awake" chemical is corticotropin-releasing hormone (CRH). It promotes the awake state and interferes with sleep, although it may play a part in REM sleep. It may also help us wake spontaneously without an alarm.

What keeps me awake?

Some nerve cells of the brain stem make the neurotransmitters serotonin and norepineph- rine. These neurotransmitters lock onto the surfaces of nerve cells in higher brain centers during the waking hours and keep them active. They block the activity of the VLPO, preventing the "sleep switch" from flipping on. When their levels fall, the VLPO triggers sleep. During sleep, neurons in the brain stem send signals that "switch off" the production of serotonin and norepinephrine.

What causes drowsiness?

Early researchers thought they might find a master "sleepiness compound" in the blood, but they failed. The fact that conjoined twins who share a circulatory system sleep at differ- ent times suggests that the substance (or maybe more than one) lies not in the body, but in the brain. In 1913, researchers gained support for this idea from experiments with dogs. Fluid extracted from around the brains of sleep-deprived dogs put well-rested dogs to sleep.

Nearly a century later, many compounds are being researched, but none has been established as the only (or even the major) sleep inducer. Part of the problem is that the same compound can have different effects in different situations. For example, the compound vasopressin keeps rats awake but increases slow-wave sleep in elderly people.

There is some evidence, however, that the compound adenosine may play an important role in initiating, maintaining, and ending sleep. Adenosine forms the backbone of adenosine triphosphate (ATP), the primary fuel molecule used in cells. ATP is an adenosine molecule with three phosphate molecules attached. The bonds that hold the phosphates to the adenosine are high-energy bonds. When they break, they release a lot of energy, which the cell uses to power its activities. The breakdown happens in the mitochondria, tiny structures inside the cell that act as the cell's power plants. There, the bonds are broken, and what's left is adenosine. Adenosine is not waste, however. It is recycled when the energy from food (in the form of the sugar glucose) is used to build up new high-energy bonds and make new ATP.

Experiments show that adenosine blocks the action of cells in the brain's arousal centers, which send signals to the body to stay awake and alert. In the brain, the areas that are the most active generate the most adenosine. Some stimulant chemicals, such as the caffeine in coffee and cola drinks, tie up the receptors on nerve cells that adenosine binds to. That may be why caffeine increases alertness and delays sleep.

It's possible that the need to replenish the ATP supply induces sleep. In humans and laboratory animals, the amount of adenosine in the brain gradually increases during the waking hours. The longer wakefulness continues, the higher the level gets and the longer and deeper the sleep that follows. Once the level of adenosine reaches a certain point, it may inhibit the TMN, or it may block signals that inhibit the brain's sleep switch, the VLPO. A reduction in activity would—in theory anyway—give neurons in those regions a chance to replenish their stock of the energy molecule ATP. Whatever the mechanism, adenosine levels drop during sleep.

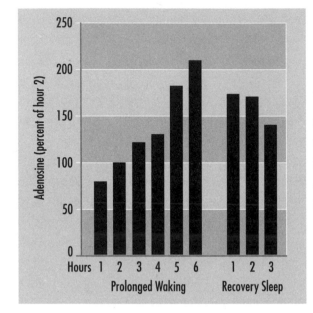

Adapted from T. Porkka-Heiskanen et al. "Adenosine: A Mediator of the Sleep-Inducing Effects of Prolonged Wakefulness." *Science* (May 23, 1997), 1266.

The longer kittens stayed awake, the higher the levels of adenosine rose in some parts of their brains. As the kittens slept, adenosine levels fell.

While substances in the brain produce sleepiness, the body must have ways to overcome their effects, at least for a time. When you are excited, stressed, or physically active, you can shake off feeling sleepy. Soldiers and extreme athletes (such as long-distance yachtsmen) can push themselves to perform on little sleep for days, even weeks. But the need for sleep catches up with everyone eventually. The longer you stay awake, the greater the urge to sleep and the less control you have over it. But time awake is not the only factor. Age, exercise, illness, drugs, and sexual maturity affect the feeling of drowsiness. So do the length of sleep on one or several previous nights and how often that sleep was interrupted.

Why do I feel sleepy after a big meal?

Popular wisdom has long answered that blood leaves the brain and flows to the gut to aid in digestion after a big meal. Evidence, however, suggests a different response. Blood flow to the brain is maintained in all healthy states. Strenuous exercise does not divert it, and neither does a hearty dinner. Instead, some investigators think a big meal may cause the gut to release hormones or send nerve impulses that affect the brain's sleep centers. Why that happens no one knows, but some researchers think body temperature may play a part. New York scientist Gary Zammit and his team fed twelve healthy men low-calorie and high-calorie lunches for four days. On two days, the men were required to stay awake. The other two days, the men could sleep. After the high-calorie meals, their body temperatures rose significantly. When the men stayed awake after big meals, their temperatures rose even higher. When sleep was allowed, it began when body temperature was highest, and then body temperature dropped sharply during sleep. It's possible that the sleep-inducing effects of a warm bath work the same way. The hot water raises body temperature and makes the person feel sleepy. Brain researchers think they may have found the area of the brain that triggers sleepiness when body temperature rises. Neurons in the basal forebrain, just in front of the body's sleep centers in the hypothalamus, become active when body temperature increases.

Why do I feel sleepy when I take allergy or cold medicines?

When you have a cold or an allergy, your immune system produces a compound called histamine. Histamine kills invading microbes, but it also irritates cells in the nose and mouth. It's the main reason for the sneezing and runny nose that come with colds and allergies. Many allergy and cold medi-cines contain antihistamines. These drugs block the action of histamine and control the symptoms. They do their job effectively, but in more places than just the nose. Histamine has another job in a very different body part. It triggers the firing of cells in the brain's alertness region, the TMN. Antihistamine drugs block histamine receptors on the surfaces of cells in the TMN, and they stop firing impulses. Rendered inactive, the neurons of the TMN cannot fire and keep you awake. So the brain's sleep centers gain the upper hand and you feel drowsy.

Why do I fall asleep and wake up at the same time every day?

In these times of all-night supermarkets and twenty-four-hour banking, it's a good thing that brain and body have several built-in, automatic, self-regulating systems for measuring and keeping time. One is the "stopwatch" that lets you judge (more or less) when five minutes have passed. Other time-keeping systems regulate monthly changes (for example, the menstrual cycle in females) and seasonal cycles (which can cause some people to feel depressed in the winter months, when light levels are low).

The most important clock for timing sleep and waking is the twenty-four-hour "circadian" (meaning "about one day") clock in the brain. The circadian clock is the suprachiasmatic nucleus (SCN) of the brain. The SCN is located in the hypothalamus, the same region where the VLPO initiates sleep and the TMN stimulates wakefulness. When the SCN is absent or damaged, animals lose their daily rhythms. If they receive "transplants" of SCN cells, they regain their daily periodicity.

Signals from the SCN travel to several brain regions, including the pineal gland. The pineal gland secretes the sleep hormone melatonin. During the day, the SCN blocks melatonin release. In the evening, the

Our brains and bodies program our behaviors in a daily, or circadian, cycle.

Adapted from Michael Smolensky and Lynne Lamberg. The Body Clock Guide to Better Health. New York: Henry Holt, 2000. With permission from Dr. Smolensky.

blocking action subsides, and the pineal releases melatonin, usually about two hours before a person's habitual bedtime. Melatonin prepares the body for sleep. It induces a feeling of drowsiness and trips the sleep switch of the VLPO.

The SCN uses chemical messengers to maintain daily rhythms. An important one is the protein hypocretin, also called orexin. During the waking hours, levels of hypocretin rise, increasing "sleep pressure," or the need to sleep. Animals kept in continuous dim red light show the normal rises and falls in hypocretin; they sleep on a more-or-less normal daily cycle. But if the SCN in animals is damaged, their hypocretin levels are low, although they rise the longer the animals stay awake. From this, researchers conclude that hypocretin regulates both the SCN and the push toward sleep that builds during wakefulness.

The SCN uses chemical messengers and nerve impulses to regulate more than sleeping and waking. It "schedules" the rise in blood pressure, heart rate, blood sugar, and the stress hormone cortisol to coincide with the beginning of the day. It also regulates the body's daily temperature cycle. Temperature rises before waking, peaks in the afternoon or early evening, and falls to its lowest between 2 and 5 A.M. Some of the SCN's daily cycling triggers illness. Its action may be the reason that heart attacks occur more frequently in the morning and asthma attacks often come at night.

How does the circadian clock work?

The neurons of the SCN do something that no other neurons can do. On their own—even growing in a laboratory dish—they create cycles of chemical and electrical activity that correspond to a twenty-four-hour day. Genes control their timed action. Some of the genes that regulate cells of the SCN have been studied. In mammals, some of the best known are called *clock, bmal, period,* and *cryptochrome.* These genes switch on and off in rhythmic cycles, creating "ripples through interconnected molecular loops." The pattern of these ripples gives the neurons of the SCN their timekeeping ability.

One such set of ripples is produced by the interaction of the *period* and *cryptochrome* genes. They cause the cells to make proteins, nicknamed *per* and *cry,* that are self-regulating. When the levels of *per* and *cry* get high enough, they "switch off" the action of *period* and *cryptochrome,* the same genes that cause their production. *Period* and *cryptochrome* are, in turn, switched on by the action of *clock* and *bmal.* Thus, in a repeating daily cycle, genes switch on and off, creating a twenty-four-hour cycle of protein production. Thus, a molecular clock drives a cellular clock that, in turn, drives an entire organism.

The SCN is not the only place where the clock genes operate. Expression of more than a thousand genes in the heart and liver tissue of mice vary in twenty-four-hour cycles. Some operate at peak levels during

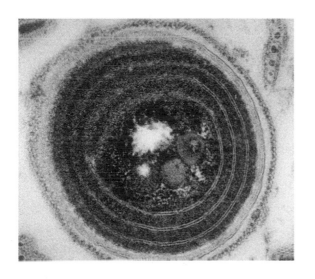

Both plants and animals have circadian clocks. The simplest known is in this blue-green alga ("pond scum") *Synechococcus.* It lacks a nucleus, but its genes turn on and off in rhythm with the twenty-four-hour day.

the day. Others swing into action only at night. All get the same messages from the SCN, but the chemical changes initiated are different. Virtually all organs in the body have their own "clocks" and operate in concert with them. Heart rate, metabolism, digestion, breathing—all cycle daily. "We have oscillators in our organs that can function independently of our oscillators in our brain," says Joseph Takahashi of Northwestern University.

Why do I have a bowel movement first thing every morning?

The need to eliminate urine and solid wastes is suppressed at night. It starts up again in the morning, under the direction of the SCN. The communication between the SCN and body organs depends on chemical messengers. No one knows for sure all the chemicals that keep body actions such as bowel movements on schedule, but one likely candidate for at least part of the job is the small protein prokineticin 2 (PK2). It is not a part of the clock itself, but it communicates clock time to other parts of the brain and body. One of its jobs is to regulate the daily rhythms of movements in the stomach and intestines. That's why bowel movements are regular, morning events and why shift workers and jet travelers so often suffer from constipation.

How does light affect the body clock?

The circadian clock of the SCN needs no external cues to make it run. It works automatically. It sticks to a twenty-four-hour day despite changes in periods of light and dark. Volunteers who stay in continuous light or dark for many days maintain a twenty-four-hour cycle of sleeping and waking. Even under the influence of large amounts of caffeine—which many coffee drinkers experience—the SCN stays accurate to within 1 percent.

That 1 percent is a small, but important, difference. It gives the SCN system enough flexibility that changes in the light-dark cycle of the environment can "reset" the clock. Such fine-tuning of the SCN happens daily, keeping the twenty-four-hour clock in synchrony with the Earth's rotation. The resetting is accomplished through the eyes, by cells called retinal ganglionic cells (RGCs). RGCs contain a light-sensitive pigment. When hit by light energy, the pigment changes chemically, triggering a nerve impulse. Impulses from RGCs travel to the SCN, where they cause the clock to be reset.

There must be more to the story than just the pigment, however. Living in constant light, mutant mice whose RGC cells don't make the pigment still keep a twenty-four-hour clock. Researchers think some other light-detection system must be affecting the SCN. One factor may be the proteins controlled by the cryptochrome genes that are known to "set" the body clocks of fruit flies. These pigments also occur in the human retina and SCN. Mice lacking *cry* proteins lose their circadian rhythms entirely.

What is jet lag?

Travel across time zones disrupts circadian rhythms. After traveling from California to New York, for example, you might set your alarm for your usual 7 A.M., but rising at that time, you'd feel tired and sluggish because you would be up at 4 A.M. California time. In short, your body would be in the Eastern time zone, but your brain would still be "set" to Pacific time. For several days, you would feel "off." With cycles of brain, digestion, body temperature, and hormonal secretion all disrupted, you might find your concentration impaired and your stomach queasy. You would feel tired, even after sleep.

The same mechanisms that fine-tune the SCN daily allow the air traveler to adjust to this "jet lag," but the resetting is slow. Exposure to light late in the evening delays the clock by about two and one-half hours a day. Light in the morning advances the clock by at most an hour and a half daily. Thus, adjustment to a new time zone can require days, even weeks.

Phase delays (flying westward to an earlier time zone) are easier to achieve than phase advances (flying eastward to a later time zone). While the SCN is resetting itself, the clocks that operate other organs, including the liver, lungs, and skeletal muscles, reset, too, but they are slower to reset than the SCN. After a while, synchrony returns, but jet travelers feel out-of-sorts until it does.

Jet lag is not just for air travelers. Its symptoms plague all-night exam crammers and party animals who keep irregular schedules of sleep and waking. People who work at night don't escape either. They continue to secrete melatonin at night, and the daily cycles of body temperature, blood pressure, and other changes remain coordinated with light and dark, not with their work schedule. For that reason, night workers and celebrants may feel constantly tired, no matter how much sleep they get during the day.

What's wrong with working nights?

The natural timing of sleep in humans results from the interaction of two factors. One is the circadian clock that "drives us" with changes in body chemistry and activity toward a pattern of activity during the day and rest at night. The other, called "homeostatic sleep pressure," is the "sleep debt" that grows with each waking hour. The longer we've gone without sleep, the drowsier we feel and the more quickly we fall asleep—light or dark, day or night. Normally, these two factors work in harmony. Both the circadian clock and homeostatic sleep pressure push toward sleep beginning somewhere between 9 and 11 P.M. and ending between 5 and 7 A.M.

For the eight million workers in the United States who regularly work at night, however, both circadian rhythms and sleep pressure are pushed out of phase, even when adequate sleep is obtained during the daylight hours. In the morning, after a night of forced alertness, sleep pressure forces sleep at the same time that the circadian clock is gearing up to promote a day of activity.

Sleep pressure diminishes when the alarm goes off in early evening, but the body is naturally pushed toward sleep at that time. A sleep debt begins to accumulate before the worker goes on the job. The result is a worker who feels tired, performs poorly, and faces serious risks to personal health.

Night workers have a greater risk of diabetes and heart disease than day workers do. "Their decreased alertness, performance, and vigilance are likely to blame for a higher rate of industrial accidents, quality-control errors on the job, injuries, and a general decline in work rate." Roadway accidents are more common in sleep-deprived truck drivers and air traffic controllers. The number and severity of accidents also increase during the night shift. One study found that medical interns who worked even one twenty-four-hour shift in a month increased their risk of a motor vehicle crash by more than 9 percent.

Shift workers who rotate between day and night work experience the greatest disruption. They take longer to get to sleep and awaken

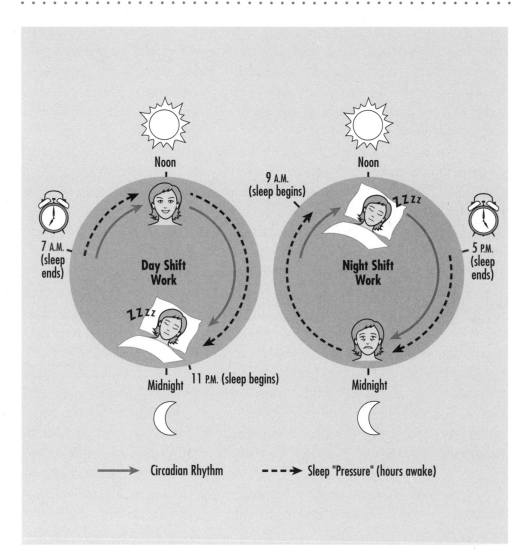

Circadian rhythms and sleep pressure work in synchrony for day workers. Night workers are not so lucky.

earlier than other workers, and they report poorer-quality sleep. These problems are more than an inconvenience. Shift workers face an increased risk of injuries and accidents, heart disease, stomach disorders, cancer, and chronic sleep disorders. Shift workers also have a higher risk of contracting common infections such as colds and flu.

Can diet or light exposure prevent or treat jet lag?

When laboratory animals are kept on low-calorie diets and strict feeding schedules, their internal clocks can be phase shifted by as much as ten hours in two days. The reset happens fastest in the liver, followed by the kidney and heart. All organs except the SCN in the brain are reset after one week. The SCN, however, remains set in accordance with the twenty-four-hour light-dark day.

These findings suggest that humans might diminish the symptoms of jet lag by eating less and at different times before travel. The SCN would still require light-dark resetting in the new time zone, but the complaints of stomach upsets and low energy might be lessened. Exactly what regimen might work best has yet to be determined, but researchers are still exploring the possibilities.

Some evidence also suggests that timed exposures to bright lights can lessen the severity of jet lag. Researchers in Chicago tested twenty-eight healthy volunteers, advancing their habitual sleep schedule by one hour a day for three days. Extra light in the morning hours advanced the volunteers' melatonin secretion by anywhere from one-half to about two hours. While that shift is small compared to the five-hour to ten-hour shift jet travelers face, it could make readjustment in the new destination quicker and easier.

Look on the shelves of most drugstores and health food stores and you'll see bottles of melatonin in pill form. Years ago, people thought melatonin might help treat or prevent jet lag, but the results were disappointing. In the largest study done so far, melatonin had no effect on jet lag. Melatonin pills can't help most people fall asleep any faster, stay asleep longer, or sleep more restfully. Melatonin pills don't help insomnia sufferers either. In fact, large amounts of melatonin or melatonin taken at the wrong time can actually injure health.

Taken under a doctor's supervision, however, melatonin can sometimes aid elderly people who produce too little melatonin or release it at the wrong time. Low doses can also help those who suffer from

Adapted from Mary A. Carskadon. "When Worlds Collide: Adolescent Need for Sleep Versus Societal Demands." *Phi Delta Kappan*, Vol. 80, No. 05 (January 1999), 348–353.

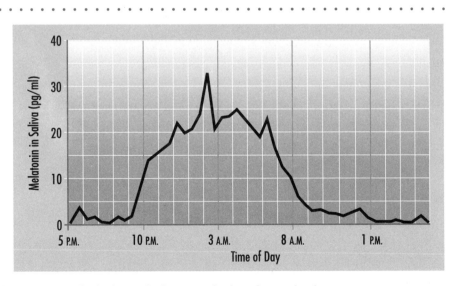

Levels of melatonin in the body are higher at night than during the day.

melatonin-deficient insomnia or "phase shift" disorders (falling asleep too early or too late). Melatonin can also assist people who are totally blind. Because their retinas do not respond to light, their circadian clocks are "free-running." They operate on a "day" that is longer or shorter than twenty-four hours. Because their SCNs cannot be reset by light, some people who are blind experience insomnia at night and sleepiness in the daytime. The right dose of melatonin taken at the right time can help them achieve a more regular daily pattern.

Is it okay to sleep with the lights on?

Not if you want to get any sleep. Even the light from a digital alarm clock can be enough to disrupt the sleep cycle. "Melatonin secretion (is) significantly inhibited by environmental light of relatively low intensity, within the range of regular room illumination," says Irina Zhdanova of Boston University Medical School. That's one reason irregular hours or shift work disrupt circadian rhythms. It's also the reason that exciting video games in the evening interfere with sleep. The light from the display terminal suppresses melatonin secretion. Fortunately, the opposite is not true. Exposure to darkness during the daytime does not trigger melatonin production. That's good news for matinee movie fans and afternoon nappers.

Why do I sleep through some noises and wake for others?

Serena Gondek and Richard Krauss at Johns Hopkins University investigated sound processing during sleep. They implanted painless electrodes in the brains of volunteers who were having brain surgery to treat their epileptic seizures. They found that a tone played during sleep activated two areas of the brain: the "primary auditory cortex," or the brain's hearing center, which is also activated during waking, and a region at the front of the brain, which is an "arousal center." That region stays vigilant during sleep, they think, screening inputs from the environment and telling the sleeper when to react.

Activity in that and other brain regions may "decide" what's worth waking up for and what's not. British researchers tested sleeping subjects with two kinds of sounds: beeps and the sleepers' names.

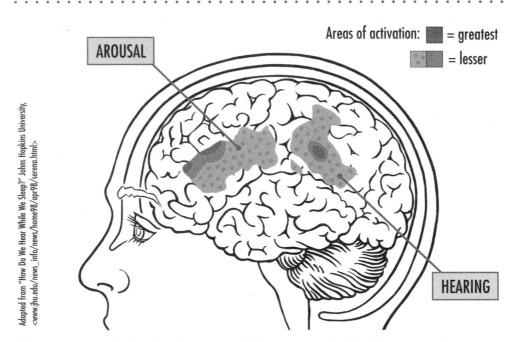

AROUSAL

HEARING

Areas of activation: ■ = greatest □ = lesser

When important sounds wake the sleeper, the brain's arousal and auditory processing centers go to work.

In response to both, the sound-sensing areas of the brain responded as expected, but the sound of the sleeper's name also activated neurons in the amygdala. The amygdala is the brain's main processing center for emotions. "Such activation appears to be part of an automatic circuit," says Harvard sleep scientist Robert Stickgold, "which first identifies emotionally salient stimuli and then initiates at least a partial arousal of the individual."

Can I listen to tapes while sleeping and learn a language?

Many studies have shown that children and adults can't do it, but one experiment found that babies can. Researchers in Finland played tapes of some hard-to-pronounce Finnish vowel sounds to forty-five newborns. EEGs made before and after the sessions showed that the infants could not distinguish between the sounds. Then the babies were divided into two groups. One group heard the vowel sounds again while they slept. The other group listened to different, easier-to-distinguish vowel sounds. When tested the following day, the babies who had heard the tricky vowel sounds as they slept could recognize them, even if the pitch was different. The babies who hadn't heard them could not.

Does sleep affect learning?

"There is growing evidence that sleep serves to consolidate memories," says Salk Institute neuroscientist Terrence Sejnowski. "Both REM sleep and slow-wave sleep may have important, but different, roles." Sejnowski thinks the brain constructs and reorganizes its circuits while we sleep. "When you make structural changes in your house, such as adding a new room, you temporarily move out so that the construction workers don't interfere with your life. During sleep, the brain is taken 'offline' so that temporary and tentative changes made during the day can be made more permanent."

How does this happen? Scientists have long associated learning with "long-term potentiation" (LTP). LTP is the process by which signals between neurons are "strengthened." By some means, neurons that have "communicated" before are more likely to communicate again in the future. Some researchers think sleep plays a part in LTP. During sleep, a series of complex chemical steps changes the action of receptors and neurotransmitters that operate in the synapse, which is the gap between neurons. It's possible that this "remodeling of synapses" during sleep is an important step in the LTP process.

Because infants spend 50 percent of their sleep time in REM, compared with adults' 20 percent, some experts think REM sleep may play a crucial role in the brain's growth and development. It may establish the neural connections that allow babies to learn new skills and master new knowledge. The process may not be confined only to the young. Interrupt their REM sleep and adults lose some recall of what they learned the day before. Also, intense study increases the need for REM sleep. Researchers at the University of Ottawa found that time spent in REM sleep increased for students who were learning a new language.

Pierre Maquet of the University College London used imaging techniques to monitor the brains of students while they learned and while they slept. Volunteers spent several hours learning to press certain buttons when they saw particular symbols on a computer screen. The students got better with practice. They got better still after they slept. Their brain scans (compared with those of untrained volunteers) showed that "sleep learning" was indeed taking place. During REM sleep, the brain's visual and movement processing centers—along with some parts of its "central dispatch" area, the thalamus—were more active in trained subjects than in untrained ones. Those same brain areas had been active during training. "These results support the hypothesis that memory traces are processed during REM sleep in humans," Maquet says.

A few experts doubt that sleep has anything to do with making memories. They say that antidepressant medications disrupt sleep but don't interfere with memory. Furthermore, patients with brain diseases or injuries sometimes have abnormal sleep cycles or lose REM sleep, but they appear to live normally otherwise. Some skeptics of the sleep-learning theory say the resemblance of REM sleep to learning may be related to REM's role in preparing the brain to wake. The increase in REM sleep after training in a new skill may be induced by the stress of training. Likewise, the deterioration in performance after sleep deprivation may be simply a stress response.

Despite those objections, evidence is accumulating to suggest that both slow-wave sleep and REM sleep play parts in learning. For example, German scientists found that slow-wave sleep (stages 3 and 4) was sufficient for learning a task, but that both slow-wave and REM sleep were needed to produce the largest increase in performance. Italian scientists taught words to young subjects, then tested their recall after undisturbed sleep and after their sleep was disrupted in different ways. As long as the normal cycling of sleep stages occurred, the subjects learned equally well. Such findings have led some sleep experts to suggest that slow-wave sleep reactivates the brain's circuits that were active during the waking-learning period. REM sleep may move new learning into long-term memory.

Can I solve problems while I sleep?

The time-honored adage "Sleep on it" may have merit. In one experiment, researchers taught volunteers two simple rules to help them put a string of eight numbers in a new order. What they didn't teach them was a third rule that made improvement in performance rapid and easy. After the initial training, the volunteers either stayed awake or slept. Those who slept were twice as likely to "dream up" the third rule than those who stayed awake.

Intellectual problem solving isn't the only kind that goes on during sleep. Our emotional problems get a helping hand, too. Mood improves after a good night's sleep, and the problem that seemed so impossible at night seems manageable the next morning. Or, as the English poet Elizabeth Barrett Browning put it, "There, that is our secret: go to sleep! You will wake, and remember, and understand."

Spinning for Science

· · · · ·

Sleeping is no mean art: for its sake one must stay awake all day.
FRIEDRICH NIETZSCHE

· · · · ·

In recent years, scientists have learned a lot about input to the SCN, the circadian timekeeper in the brain that schedules and regulates the body's daily, regular, rhythmic changes, including sleeping and waking. Less well understood have been the SCN's outputs—that is, how it sends the signals that control daily, rhythmic changes in other organs.

To learn more about the outputs, Charles Weitz and a team of researchers in Boston experimented with hamsters and mice. In the wild, these animals hunt for food at night. In the laboratory, they normally run their exercise wheels at night. This wheel-running behavior must be under the control of the SCN, Weitz reasoned. Some molecule must leave the SCN at night, telling the body and brain to become active. The team knew about more than twenty different peptides (small protein molecules) secreted by the SCN, but they didn't know what the peptides do. To find out, they infused the test animals' SCNs with each of the peptides, then observed wheel-running behavior. In this way, they discovered the first "SCN output signal" known in mammals: transforming growth factor alpha (TGF-α).

The animals with high levels of TGF-α in their SCNs remained healthy in every way, but they

In captivity, hamsters run their exercise wheels throughout the night.

stopped running on their wheels at night. When Weitz's team measured the natural levels of TGF-α in their control, or untreated, animals, they found that TGF-α levels were high during the day and low at night. From this result, Weitz's team concluded that TGF-α naturally inhibits activity during the day. When its levels drop at night, the animal becomes active.

Weitz knew that a brain area near the SCN, the subparaventricular zone (SPZ), controls daily run-

ning rhythms. On the surfaces of cells in that brain region, he found receptors for TGF-α. He reasoned that TGF-α molecules fit into those receptors like keys fit into locks. When the keys are in place, because TGF-α levels are high, the neurons of the SPZ don't fire, and the animal doesn't run. But when fewer keys are around, the cells are free to fire and initiate wheel running. This hypothesis was supported by an experiment with a drug known to block those receptors. When test animals got it, they ran their wheels less.

Mutant animals with faulty TGF-α receptors run their wheels during the day more than normal animals do. The mutant animals behave abnormally in other ways, too. Normal animals stop running their wheel at night when the lights are turned on. This response is called masking. Masking is the brain's way of overriding activity signals when danger such as a predator approaches and activity would be risky. Weitz's mutant animals were poor maskers. They kept going even when the lights came on. The signal for masking behavior seems to go directly to the SPZ from the RGCs, cells in the retina of the eye that allow light to reset the SCN. Researchers doubt that TGF-α is the only substance that regulates the timing of wheel-running behavior, so they are looking for other chemicals that get into the act.

CHAPTER FOUR

21 QUESTIONS

ABOUT SLEEP DISORDERS

The two best physicians of them all—Dr. Laughter and Dr. Sleep.

• GREGORY DEAN JR. •

What are the most common sleep disorders?

The National Institutes of Health estimate that sleep-related problems affect fifty to seventy million Americans. They define three categories of sleep problems:

+ **Sleep restriction:** As a result of lifestyle, work schedules, or choice, many people of all ages get less sleep than they need to function effectively during waking hours.

+ **Primary sleep disorders:** More than seventy primary sleep disorders are known. The most common are insomnia, sleep apnea, narcolepsy, and restless legs syndrome. About half of the people who have sleep disorders get no diagnosis and no treatment.

✦ **Secondary sleep disorders**: People who have a chronic disease or substance abuse problem may lose sleep as a result. Conditions that bring on sleep loss include psychiatric conditions such as depression and anxiety, painful diseases such as arthritis, and alcoholism and drug abuse.

What is insomnia and how is it treated?

Insomnia has four forms: (1) difficulty falling asleep, (2) waking too early and not being able to get back to sleep, (3) waking frequently, and (4) waking feeling tired.

About one in every six adults reports some form of insomnia. More than half of them are women. Although the prevalence of insomnia increases with age, it's not a disease of later life. Among young adults ages nineteen to twenty-nine, two-thirds report a symptom of insomnia occurring a few nights a week. Only 44 percent of those past retirement age report such a pattern.

Insomnia can have either physical or psychological causes. Pain provokes sleeplessness among people who are injured, sick, hospitalized, or who suffer from painful conditions such as arthritis or rheumatism. Other causes include breathing difficulty during sleep, uncontrollable movements of the arms and legs, use of sleep-disrupting alcohol and drugs (including caffeine in coffee and soft drinks), and digestive complaints such as heartburn. Still, the most common cause of insomnia is life events. We lose sleep when we worry about family, health, work, or school.

Sometimes, the cause of insomnia is obvious and simply remedied.

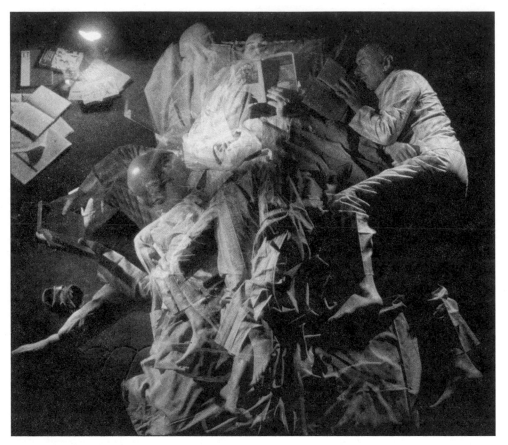

This is a multiple-exposure image showing a man with insomnia trying to fall asleep. His nights consist of tossing and turning punctuated by bouts of reading.

Solving a life problem or learning skills in stress management can relieve worries that stop sleep from coming. A room that is too hot or too cold can interfere with sleep, as can an uncomfortable mattress or pillow. For those who have trouble relaxing, warm baths, hot drinks, and quiet reading or music can help bring on sleep. Regular bedtimes, avoiding naps late in the day, and giving up caffeine often help. Repetitive activities such as knitting or deep breathing help some people with insomnia get to sleep. If the need to urinate is disturbing sleep, drinking no liquids after dinner can solve the problem. If pain is the cause of insomnia, pain-relieving medicines can be the answer. In some cases, doctors prescribe sleep-promoting drugs, but they are not for long-term use.

Persistent or severe cases of insomnia may be relieved through biofeedback. Using biofeedback techniques, patients can listen to computer-generated tones that tell them when their brain waves (as recorded in an EEG) are entering stage 1 sleep patterns. This feedback helps some people with insomnia learn to relax into sleep. Also effective for some is cognitive therapy, in which patients learn specific techniques for reducing anxiety and promoting sleep onset. What does not work is counting sheep. Imagining a peaceful scene like a beach or a waterfall will put you to sleep twenty minutes faster than counting sheep will.

Is snoring anything to worry about? "Snoring is a huge red flag," says neurologist and sleep specialist Pat Burns, of the Sleep Medicine Center in Kalispell, Montana. Snoring reliably predicts daytime tiredness, regardless of whether any sleep disorder has been diagnosed, he says. Snoring is also a major symptom of sleep apnea (see next question).

Before we look at the health risks associated with snoring, let's define what snoring actually is. Air whizzing over the bumps and lumps in the throat and windpipe creates the sounds of snoring. It happens during inhalation, exhalation, or both. A blockage of the nose from allergies or from a deformity of the nasal septum (the cartilage

Some famous snorers who may have had sleep apnea include composer Johannes Brahms (shown here), Britain's World War II prime minister Winston Churchill, and the former president of the United States, Grover Cleveland.

that separates the two sides of the nose) can cause it. When the snorer takes a breath, the tongue, soft palate (at the back of the mouth), uvula, and throat may all vibrate, making a raspy, fluttering noise.

About 25 percent of men and 15 percent of women snore. In one survey, 37 percent of adults said they snore frequently. About 10 percent said they experience problems breathing during sleep. Chronic and severe snoring, especially in the young with no other sleep disorders, is associated with high blood pressure. High blood pressure, also called hypertension, is a major risk factor for heart disease and stroke. Australian researcher Matthew Naughton has found that snorers also face a greater risk of congestive heart failure:

They [snorers] develop periods of pausing to their breathing and often fragmented sleep, and fragmented sleep or sleep deprivation can lead to stress on the heart in itself. Secondly, when people snore and arouse from sleep, . . . the blood pressure is surging up and down, . . . the heart is having to work against upstream resistance. And another factor that occurs during the night, in snorers, is that their oxygen levels are falling, . . . and the heart muscle gets stiff. It doesn't relax and fill easily. So the heart doesn't pump as effectively.

Naughton says people who snore more than three times a week, snore loudly, or experience excessive daytime sleepiness should see a physician. Some snorers can cure themselves by losing weight, getting their allergies treated, getting more sleep, or giving up cigarettes and alcohol. Others may need to sleep with a mouthpiece that moves the jaw into a position that prevents vibration of the soft palate and uvula at the back of the mouth. Those structures can be surgically removed or reduced in cases of chronic, severe snoring. Alternatives are to stiffen the tissues of the soft palate using radio waves, injections, or surgical lesions.

What is sleep apnea and how is it treated?

Sleep apnea is a disorder of breathing. The person with apnea breathes normally when awake, but during sleep, the walls of the airway constrict. The sleeper inhales, but cannot take in enough air. Airflow is blocked for as little as ten seconds or as long as a full minute, while the sleeper struggles to breathe. Declining blood oxygen levels may wake the sleeper, but more often the arousal is so slight, the sleeper is never aware of it.

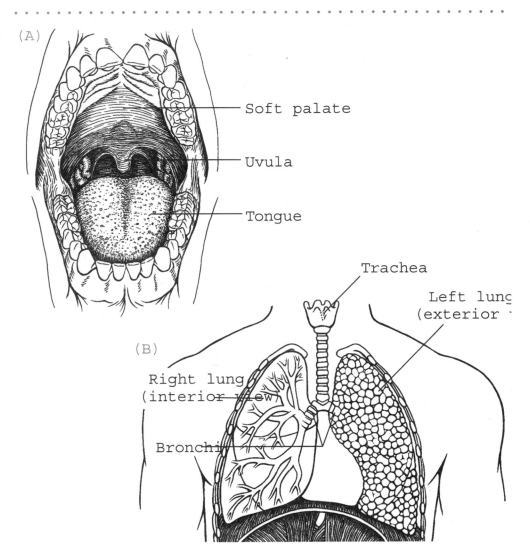

(A) Vibration of the uvula and soft palate in the back of the mouth causes snoring sounds.
(B) Disorders of airflow to the trachea and bronchi into the lungs cause sleep apnea.

The arousal does, however, open the airway enough for air to rush in, creating a loud, snoring sound. Sleep returns immediately, and the apnea sufferer may be unaware of having awakened hundreds of times each night. Nevertheless, the result is loss of sleep, which can lead to daytime sleepiness, difficulty in paying attention, and behavioral problems. This obstructive sleep apnea is the most common reason why people go to sleep laboratories.

Sleep apnea runs in some families, and may be associated with the structure of the jaw or the size and shape of the respiratory passages. It can occur if the neurons that control breathing malfunction during sleep, but the most common cause is a narrowing of the air passages. The point of the constriction can be anywhere from the back of the nose and throat to the point where the windpipe (trachea) divides into the two tubes (bronchi) that lead to the lungs. The constriction is often caused by extra tissue in the region between the base of the tongue and the Adam's apple.

Overweight increases the risk of apnea, because fat accumulates around the walls of the breathing tubes. Alcohol and sedatives also contribute to sleep apnea. They depress the central nervous system and relax muscles of the airway. Age is also a factor. In children, big tonsils and enlarged adenoids may be to blame. In older people, the tissues of the air passages may slacken, making them more likely to close during inhalation. Some abnormalities in the brain have also been found. Patients with too few acetylcholine-producing neurons in the brain stem have the most interruptions of their breathing during sleep.

Whatever the cause, frequent awakenings leave people with sleep apnea tired, irritable, and sad. Because sleep apnea deprives the brain of oxygen, people who have it may complain of headaches and difficulty concentrating. The disorder is also linked to high blood pressure, diabetes, and an increased risk of heart attacks and stroke. Patients with severe, untreated sleep apnea are two to three times more likely to have automobile accidents than the general population. Severe, untreated cases may result in sudden death due to respiratory arrest during sleep.

About fifteen million Americans have sleep apnea—three-quarters of them men and only 10 percent of them receiving treatment. (Some experts say the numbers are much greater. Many people have sleep apnea and don't know it.) People with symptoms and risk factors—including loud snoring, obesity, and excessive daytime sleepiness—can be diagnosed by a sleep specialist using a test called polysomnography.

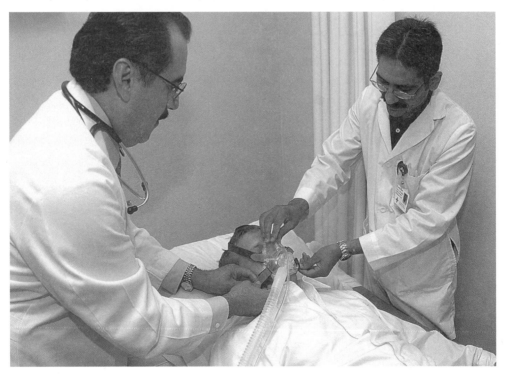

Sleep apnea can be treated with continuous positive airway pressure (CPAP).

This test records brain waves, heartbeat, and breathing during an entire night. (See "One Night in a Sleep Lab," page 124.)

If sleep apnea is diagnosed, many people are treated with continuous positive airway pressure (CPAP). The CPAP mask fits over the nose. Connected to a blower, it forces air through the nostrils and into the breathing passages. The pressure keeps the airway open and oxygen flowing, so that the patient does not need to wake in order to breathe. Although the device appears uncomfortable, sleep apnea patients soon adapt to it. And it saves lives. For example, sleep apnea patients treated with CPAP have fewer vehicular accidents than those who are not treated.

What is narcolepsy and how is it treated?

Narcolepsy is a disorder characterized by sudden, unpredictable onsets of sleep. People who have narcolepsy fall into brief periods of deep sleep—sometimes as many as twenty a day—even if they have slept well the night before. People with narcolepsy go directly into REM sleep, skipping sleep stages 1 through 4. Their "sleep attacks" can be as short as thirty seconds or as long as thirty minutes. Perhaps half of all people with narcolepsy experience vivid hallucinations associated with sleep onset. A similar number may experience temporary paralysis just before falling asleep or when waking. Strong emotion or excitement triggers cataplexy in some people who have narcolepsy. Muscles go limp, and the person with narcolepsy collapses, with arms and legs paralyzed, while still conscious and aware.

In 1999, Emmanuel Mignot and his colleagues at Stanford University in California discovered a gene associated with narcolepsy. Studying narcoleptic dogs, they found a mutant gene that left the dogs' brain cells devoid of receptors for hypocretin (also called orexin). Hypocretin is an important neurotransmitter. It stimulates the brain's arousal centers, maintaining wakefulness. Without it, sleep onset is sudden and uncontrollable.

A genetic defect of the hypocretin system has been found in some, but not all, people with narcolepsy. In some of them, hypocretin is not made in adequate amounts. Others lack, as did Mignot's dogs, receptors for hypocretin on their cell surfaces. Still others lack the cells that make hypocretin. It's possible that the immune system mistakenly attacks and destroys them.

Narcolepsy affects about one out of every two thousand people worldwide. It is more common in men than in women, and often begins in the twenties, although it may begin in childhood. "Narcolepsy is not a rare disorder," says Michael Silber, a neurologist at the Mayo Clinic. "In a community of one million, about five hundred people will have the disorder at any time, and about fourteen new cases will develop every year."

Narcolepsy can't be cured, but it can be treated with stimulant drugs that promote wakefulness, naps that alleviate fatigue, and drugs that activate hypocretin-containing neurons and suppress REM sleep.

Is daytime sleepiness a sleep disorder?

It is if it's severe enough to interfere with normal daytime activities. It even has a name: excessive daytime sleepiness (EDS). People with EDS feel an overwhelming urge to sleep during the day. They frequently doze, nap, or fall asleep in situations where they need or want to be fully awake and alert. The National Institutes of Health say young adults ages twelve to fifteen face a high risk of problem sleepiness.

EDS is more than an inconvenience. It's dangerous when driving a car or operating machinery. EDS can affect those who get enough sleep at night—or who think they do. It can also be a symptom of some other sleep disorder.

DO YOU HAVE EDS?

Use the Epworth Sleepiness Scale to determine whether your daytime drowsiness is excessive. If your score is 6 or less, you're probably getting enough sleep. A score of 9 or above means you should see a sleep specialist right away.

SCORING:
0 = would never doze
1 = slight chance of dozing
2 = moderate chance of dozing
3 = high chance of dozing

SITUATION:
- Sitting and reading
- Watching television
- Sitting quietly after lunch
- In a car, while stopped for a few minutes in traffic
- Lying down to rest in the afternoon when circumstances permit
- Sitting and talking to someone
- As a passenger in a car for an hour without a break
- Sitting inactive in a public place; for example, a theater or meeting

---

Depression is a disorder of mood. It's a feeling of sadness and despair that lasts for two weeks or more and is so severe that it interferes with family, school, work, and social activities. An imbalance of neurotransmitters in the brain causes depression, so it's no surprise that sleep disturbances go along with it. In one study, depressed women recalled fewer dreams, had significantly shorter dream length, and displayed less anger in their dreams. They also had fewer characters in their dreams and especially fewer strangers. Among young people, insomnia appears in 75 percent of depression cases. Hypersomnia (sleeping too much) is noted in 25 percent of cases, and it occurs more frequently after puberty.

Depressed people often shift their schedules, going to bed later and rising later, too. Waking very early in the morning and being unable to return to sleep is a symptom of depression in some people. Another is the premature onset of REM sleep. Normally, sleep stages 1 through 4 last eighty to one hundred minutes before REM begins. Among depressed people, REM sleep may begin in as little as fifteen to thirty minutes after the onset of sleep.

REM sleep disruption may predict depression before other symptoms develop. In one study, California scientists studied a group of teens, average age fifteen, whose REM periods occurred early in the sleep cycle. They found that 80 percent of those who entered REM too soon had developed signs of depression seven years later.

"Nobody knows if depression causes insomnia or vice versa—it's very circular," says David Dinges, a psychiatrist at the University of Pennsylvania School of Medicine. Nonetheless, for many patients, treating one improves the other. It's important to see a physician if you feel depressed.

Can the
circadian clock
malfunction?

Yes, and shifts in the body's daily rhythms can disrupt work and play.

One disorder of the circadian clock is delayed sleep phase syndrome (DSPS). People with DSPS can't fall asleep as early as their jobs or social lives demand, and they have trouble rising as early as they need to. They toss and turn for hours trying to fall asleep, but sleep won't come until the early-morning hours. Once asleep, the person with DSPS sleeps normally, going through the usual sleep stages and temperature fluctuations, but rising when the alarm clock rings is difficult.

Since everyone has occasional problems getting to sleep, DSPS is diagnosed only if the problem persists for more than six months. It is most common among young adults and adolescents, affecting perhaps 7 percent of those ages twelve to twenty. Sleep interventions are used to treat the condition, the goal being to advance the brain's twenty-four-hour clock, the SCN.

Chronotherapy is one such intervention. It's a systematic approach to changing sleeping and waking times in order to reset the biological clock. Also, bright light in the morning may help reset the SCN to a more normal day length, and doses of melatonin given in the evening initiate sleep earlier.

Advanced sleep phase syndrome (ASPS) is the opposite of DSPS. The individual with ASPS feels sleepy earlier than most people do, typically between 7 and 9 P.M. Early-morning waking may occur between 2 and 5 A.M. Sleep in between is normal. The disorder may result from a reduced capacity to respond to daily cues that reset the circadian clock or a shortening of its period to less than twenty-four hours. One form of ASPS is inherited from one parent. The gene for it is located on chromosome 2. ASPS is much rarer than DSPS. It usually occurs in

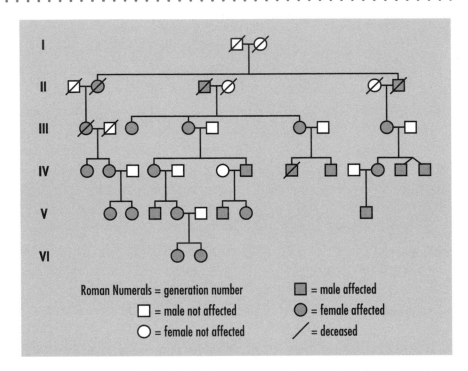

Adapted from K. L. Toh, C. R. Jones, Y. He et al. "An hPer2 Phosphorylation Site Mutation in Familial Advanced Sleep Phase Syndrome." *Science* (February 9, 2001), 1040–1043.

I

II

III

IV

V

VI

Roman Numerals = generation number

☐ = male not affected

◯ = female not affected

■ = male affected

● = female affected

╱ = deceased

Either the mother or the father of this family's first generation (I) must have had the gene for ASPS. Find the symbols for their twenty-one living descendants who are early risers.

mature people, affecting about 1 percent of middle-aged people and a higher percentage of the elderly.

The treatment is much the same as for DSPS, including chronotherapy, bright light, and melatonin, but administered at different times. Exposure to bright light occurs in the evening to delay the onset of natural melatonin secretion. Melatonin taken in the early morning can extend sleep periods.

Another circadian disorder is described simply as irregular sleep-wake patterns. Sleeping and waking occur at unpredictable times of the day and night, in episodes of no more than four hours. This disorder is rare. It is usually seen only in people with long-term illnesses who require months of bed rest or those with brain injuries or diseases that damage the SCN. Light, melatonin, and chronotherapy are used to reestablish the normal eight-hour sleep period.

A fourth circadian disorder is the non-twenty-four-hour sleep-wake disorder. It is extremely rare, affecting only those few individuals whose body clocks do not operate on a twenty-four-hour cycle. Their body clocks are said to be "free-running." They typically delay sleep and wake times by one or two hours daily. People who are totally blind are most likely to develop this unusual disorder. It affects perhaps as many as three in every four blind people. Melatonin treatment may help them regulate their cycles.

What is periodic limb movement syndrome (PLMS) and how is it treated?

Twitching of the legs or arms during the night, or PLMS, is a common, but little understood, problem. The condition seems to be more common in women, especially during pregnancy, and in patients with kidney or liver disease or back injuries. Although rare in childhood, PLMS may be associated with some cases of hyperactivity and learning, emotional, and social problems.

Some people with PLMS are unaware of their movements and do not have disturbed sleep, but those who share their bed are awakened by it. Others with PLMS wake when they move, and they may take sedative drugs to relieve insomnia or EDS. PLMS occurs in 80 percent of people who have restless legs syndrome.

What is restless
legs syndrome and
how is it treated?

If creeping, crawling, tingling, or tugging sensations forced you to move your legs constantly just to get some relief, how well would you sleep? For the four million Americans who experience such feelings when they sit or lie down, the answer is obvious. The disorder, called restless legs syndrome (RLS), usually affects the calves, but the discomfort, even pain, can also move into the thighs, ankles, and sometimes arms. Symptoms may develop during any sedentary activity, such as sitting at a desk or riding in a car. Relief comes with movement or with rubbing or massaging the legs. The symptoms get worse in the evening and at night. Because the discomfort keeps them awake at night, people who have RLS are often chronically sleep deprived.

RLS affects one in ten people over sixty-five and 3 percent of those under thirty. In children, RLS is sometimes explained away as "grow-

Adapted from the National Sleep Foundation "Sleep in America" poll, 2001.

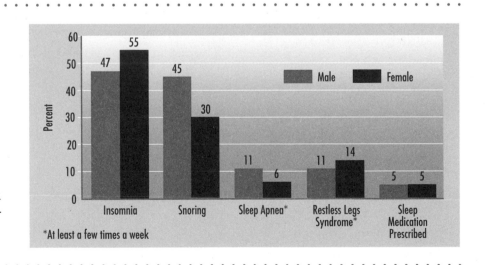

ing pains." Symptoms are more common among women during pregnancy and tend to disappear after the pregnancy ends. RLS also shows up more often among people who have diabetes or an underactive thyroid gland. About half of all cases of RLS begin in middle age. The other half begin in childhood or early adult life. Onset before age thirty is inherited, as a result of a dominant gene from one parent. Most cases that develop later in life are not inherited, but a tendency toward RLS runs in families.

In 2003, researchers at Pennsylvania State University found what they think might cause RLS. In an area of the brain called the substantia nigra, they found cells that don't get enough iron. The cells are not damaged, and the diet is not iron-deficient, but the cells lack the receptors on their outer membranes that should bind iron atoms. Enough iron gets into the cells to keep them alive, but not enough for them to function as they should. Researcher James Connor says that misfiring of the nerve cells because of iron deficiency may be responsible for the creepy-crawly sensation in the legs. This finding may also explain why some people get temporary relief from their symptoms from iron supplements prescribed by a physician. It may also explain why dopamine drugs are effective treatments. The iron-deficient cells normally make dopamine, and iron is used in making that neurotransmitter.

Many people get adequate relief from their symptoms with hot baths, heating pads, ice packs, sore-muscle creams, and massage. Exercise often helps, although strenuous activity close to bedtime may make symptoms worse. Avoiding alcohol, tobacco, and caffeine helps some people. Others get relief from vitamin and iron supplements. Another treatment is transcutaneous electric nerve stimulation. A mild electric current stimulates the muscles of the legs for fifteen minutes or more before bedtime. Doctors sometimes prescribe sleep aids, pain relievers, and other drugs to help people with RLS. The most effective drugs are those that affect the levels and action of the brain's neurotransmitter dopamine. They relieve symptoms in 99 percent of the patients who use them.

What is REM behavior disorder (RBD) and how is it treated?

"Normally in REM sleep," explains Brad Boeve, a neurologist at the Mayo Clinic in Rochester, Minnesota, "almost every muscle in your body is paralyzed and you don't move. Therefore, when you have a dream, there's no excessive activity and no potential for injury. In this [REM behavior] disorder, for reasons we don't fully understand yet, . . . normal paralysis is lost, and people appear to act out their dreams. Sometimes, they're pleasant dreams. Usually, they're nightmarish, violent dreams with the person being chased or attacked by something or someone. So, they try to defend themselves or fight against it, leading to punching and kicking. They can injure themselves by jumping out of bed, striking the bedposts or diving out of bed. As for their bed partners—they often get injured."

RBD arises because something interferes with the normal signal system in the brain that shuts down spinal nerve action, causing paralysis of major muscles during sleep. RBD may have something to do with neurotransmitters in the brain. In one study, patients with the fewest dopamine-producing neurons in one area of their brains had the worst RBD symptoms. For reasons not well understood, many RBD patients have an impaired sense of smell.

Whatever the cause, between 80 and 90 percent of those who have it are male. It can occur along with some other neurological diseases, so it's important to see a doctor if RBD symptoms appear. Antiseizure drugs used to help people who have epilepsy can alleviate RBD in some patients. Melatonin helps some, but it can worsen symptoms in others.

What is sleep paralysis and is it a sleep disorder? During normal sleep, the major voluntary muscles of the arms and legs are paralyzed. We don't and can't move or speak as we sleep, but we don't know it. When we become aware of it—usually during the transition time between REM sleep and waking—we experience "sleep paralysis" or the feeling of being immobilized in bed, unable to call for help. About half of us have an episode once or twice in our lifetimes, and perhaps as many as 6 percent of us have frequent episodes. Sleep paralysis usually starts in the teen years, and it's relatively rare after age thirty. Nevertheless, episodes are common for some, such as people who regularly get too little sleep. It's so common among nurses who work night shifts that it's called "night nurse paralysis."

In most cases, sleep paralysis passes and is forgotten. Some people, however, experience hallucinations along with the feeling of immobility. The half-asleep person may imagine an evil spirit or monster sitting on the chest or pinning the sleeper down. Shadows in a dark room may seem solid and evoke feelings of panic or dread. So common is the nightmarish quality of sleep paralysis that some researchers think it is the major reason that some people believe they have been possessed by a demon or abducted by aliens. As full wakefulness is achieved, the paralysis ends, but fear and anxiety may persist. Sleep paralysis is not considered a sleep disorder. Its risks arise mostly from the lingering fear it can engender. Severe cases can be treated with antidepressant drugs.

Are sleeping pills a good idea?

For a few days, under the supervision of a physician, they may be, but over the long haul, they spell trouble. They do the opposite of what they are meant to do. They disrupt normal sleep patterns and increase symptoms

DRUGS THAT PROMOTE SLEEP*

CATEGORY	HOW THEY WORK	EXAMPLES: GENERIC (BRAND NAME)	NOTES
Sedative-hypnotic medications: benzodiazepines	Slow the action of the central nervous system.	flurazepam (Dalmane) triazolam (Halcion)	Because of the potential for dependency and abuse, these drugs are no longer the "first-line" treatment for insomnia.
Sedative-hypnotic medications: nonbenzodiazepines	Depress the central nervous system, causing drowsiness and reducing alertness.	zolpidem (Ambien) zaleplon (Sonata)	Lose effectiveness after a few days or weeks.
Over-the-counter sleep aids	Most contain antihistamines that block the action of histamine, a neuro-transmitter important to wakefulness.	Nytol, Sominex, Sleep-Eze	Should not be taken for more than a few days. They can actually make sleep problems worse.

CATEGORY	HOW THEY WORK	EXAMPLES: GENERIC (BRAND NAME)	NOTES
Sedating antidepressants	Used to evaluate mood and alleviate anxiety, these drugs promote sleep as a side effect.	trazodone (Desyrel) amitriptyline (Elavil) doxepin (Sinequan)	May have more unwanted side effects than sedative-hypnotic medications.
Herbal remedies	Unknown, untested	valerian, chamomile, kava kava	"Natural" does not necessarily mean "safe and effective." Many claims for herbal drugs have not been evaluated in scientific tests.

* Categories and examples from the American Insomnia Association. Drug information from MedlinePlus, a service of the National Library of Medicine and the National Institutes of Health.

of insomnia. Some are addictive, and stopping them can bring on anxiety, nightmares, and persistent sleeplessness. Used along with alcohol, they can be deadly.

How do "street drugs" affect sleep?

We'll consider just a few in answering this question.

The active compound in marijuana is delta-9 tetrahydrocannabinol (THC). THC interferes with neurotransmitters and produces changes in the brain-wave patterns recorded on the EEG. Using marijuana increases total sleep time, although the time spent in slow-wave sleep does not change. Marijuana reduces REM sleep, which may explain why users report feeling tired when awake. Stopping marijuana use leads to a "rebound effect," in which REM sleep periods increase.

Cocaine is a stimulant of the central nervous system (CNS). It produces feelings of happiness followed by despair. It produces those effects by interfering with the neurotransmitter dopamine in the brain. Dopamine is an important regulator of both wakefulness and body movement. Cocaine reduces both stage 3 and stage 4 slow-wave sleep and REM sleep.

"Speed" and other amphetamines are strong CNS stimulants. They activate the brain's wakefulness centers and produce changes in brain-wave patterns. Like cocaine, they reduce both slow-wave and REM sleep. They retard sleep onset and sleep maintenance. Amphetamines can be successfully used under a doctor's supervision to treat narcolepsy.

Heroin suppresses breathing, movement, and thinking. It suppresses sleep stages 3 and 4 and REM sleep and causes frequent waking from sleep. Withdrawal symptoms include intense pain, runny nose, and a large increase in the fraction of sleep time spent in REM sleep. Terrifying nightmares often accompany this REM "rebound" in heroin addicts.

By the way, drugs don't have to be illegal to impair sleep. Caffeinated drinks such as coffee and colas cause insomnia. So do some diet pills for weight loss and some decongestants taken for colds and allergies. The nicotine in tobacco interferes with sleep. Smokers often sleep lightly, getting less deep sleep (stages 3 and 4) and less REM sleep than nonsmokers do. Nicotine withdrawal may wake a smoker in the night.

Is alcohol a good way to get to sleep? Despite what many people think, an alcoholic drink before bed is no cure for insomnia. Although it brings on sleep more quickly, its effects soon wear off. The rebound effect is awakening within two to four hours, feeling dehydrated, headachey, and unable to return to sleep. Alcohol relaxes the muscles in the airway and interferes with breathing during sleep. As a result, drinkers often snore, and if they have sleep apnea, their symptoms grow worse.

How dangerous is drowsy driving? The National Highway Traffic Safety Administration says fatigue or sleepiness is the main cause of at least 100,000 road accidents in the United States each year. More than fifteen hundred Americans die in these accidents, and another forty thousand are injured annually. More than half of those crashes involve drivers younger than twenty-six.

The riskiest roads are long, boring, rural highways, where nearly a third of the fatal crashes are caused by a driver who falls asleep. Young male drivers are at greater risk than older drivers and females. In North Carolina, researchers found that more than half of the fall-asleep crashes involved people under twenty-five, and more than three-quarters were males. Shift workers face a higher risk, too. Nearly a third of them have a fatigue-related accident each year. People in certain occupations, such as truck drivers and traveling sales representatives, face a greater risk, too.

Sleepy drivers cause more accident fatalities than drunk drivers do. Staying awake seventeen to nineteen hours—not very unusual in our get-up-early-stay-up-late society—can reduce reaction times and driv-

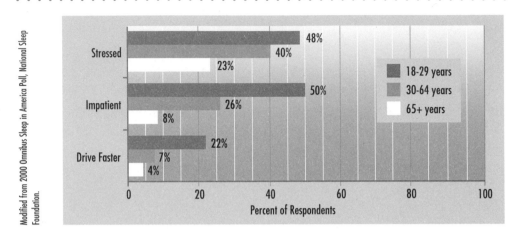

Modified from 2000 Omnibus Sleep in America Poll, National Sleep Foundation.

Drivers say drowsiness makes them feel stressed and impatient. They also drive faster. Younger drivers are more vulnerable than older drivers.

ing ability as much as or more than driving after drinking. Researchers at Brown Medical School used driving simulators to test fifteen young doctors working as residents in hospitals.

When tired from working long hours, the doctors lost some of their ability to maintain a lane position and a constant speed. Their driving performance was as bad as *or worse than* when they had drunk enough alcohol to bring their blood alcohol to 0.04 to 0.06 percent. (Most states define a driver as being legally drunk at 0.08 percent.)

In a similar study, Australian researchers administered a computerized test to measure the hand-eye coordination of forty adults. In one experiment, the subjects stayed awake from 8 A.M. on one day until noon on the next. In the other experiment, they drank about 10 to 15 grams (about half an ounce) of alcohol every thirty minutes until their blood alcohol concentration reached 0.10 percent. Staying awake impaired performance just as much as alcohol did.

"It only takes three to four seconds to fall asleep into a drowsy driving crash," says Judith Owens, a doctor at Brown University Medical School. To avoid one, don't drive when drowsy. Don't drive all night or long distances without rest. Early afternoon driving is risky, too, if you normally feel drowsy at that time. Avoid driving alone, or on long, rural, boring roads. Don't drive when drinking or

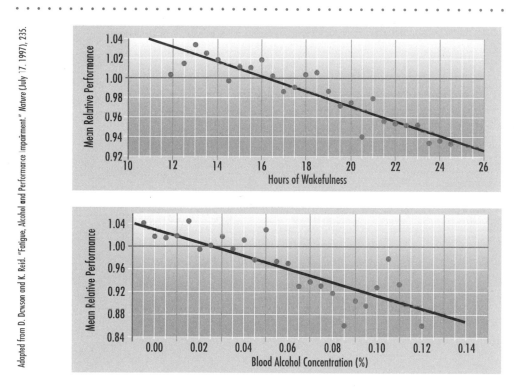

Adapted from D. Dawson and K. Reid. "Fatigue, Alcohol and Performance impairment." *Nature* (July 17. 1997), 235.

On a test of hand-eye coordination, drowsy people (graph a) did worse than people who had been drinking (graph b).

taking medication (such as allergy or cold preparations) that may make you drowsy. Avoid driving between the hours of 2 A.M. and 5 A.M. Your risk of a crash is five times greater at those times. Opening a window, playing the radio, or running the air conditioner will not keep a drowsy driver awake. Pull over into a safe rest area and take a nap.

In 2003, the New Jersey state legislature passed a landmark bill nicknamed "Maggie's Law," named after twenty-year-old Maggie McDonnell, who was killed by a driver who fell asleep at the wheel. The law established fatigued driving as recklessness under the vehicular homicide statutes of that state. It was the first bill in the nation that specifically addressed the issue of tired drivers, but it's not the only state where sleep-deprived drivers are held responsible for their actions. Under existing laws, drivers everywhere can and are being prosecuted for driving without adequate rest.

TOO TIRED TO DRIVE?

You know you are too tired to drive if you

- Can't remember the last few miles you have driven
- Drift out of your lane or hit a rumble strip
- Find that your thoughts are wandering or disconnected
- Yawn repeatedly
- Have trouble keeping your eyes open or focused
- Drive too close to the car in front of you
- Miss traffic signs or signals
- Have to consciously lift your drooping head
- Jerk your car back into your lane

Sleepwalking is fairly common in children and dangerous to them only because of the risk of injury. Some of its signs are partial waking, open eyes, a dazed expression, sitting up in bed or moving from the bed, and confusion or disorientation if awakened. Although sleepwalkers can avoid objects in their path, even perform complex tasks, there is no evidence that higher brain functions are working as they do when the brain is awake.

Childhood sleepwalking is most common between ages five and twelve. About three in every twenty children sleepwalk, most of them boys. Sleepwalking usually occurs during sleep stages 3 and 4. Episodes can last from thirty seconds to thirty minutes or longer and may occur more than once a night. There are no lingering aftereffects. The sleepwalker does not remember anything that happened.

"Sleepwalking in children decreases with time and does not represent any serious psychological problems," says Richard Ferver, an expert on children's sleep. Most children outgrow sleepwalking by the time they are fourteen. Doctors advise concerned parents never to punish a child for sleepwalking and not to frighten or confuse the child with an attempt at awakening. They recommend gently guiding the child back to bed without awakening. The most important thing is the safety of the environment. Remove potentially dangerous objects that the child could bump into or fall over.

Only 2 percent of adults are sleepwalkers. In adults, sleepwalking involves violence and injury more often than in children, and it may overlap with REM behavior disorder (RBD). It may also be associated with alcohol abuse, sleep apnea, or mental health problems. Some specialists think the adult form is inherited and possibly related to the immune system. Sleepwalking can disappear if an underlying cause such as restless legs syndrome, sleep apnea, or PLMS is treated.

What causes sleeptalking?

Sleeptalking is a misnomer. For most of us, it is better described as sleepmumbling, although we occasionally utter understandable words and sentences. Like sleepwalking, sleeptalking is most common in children, but adults can sleeptalk, too. Some experts say everyone has talked during sleep on some occasion. Most sleeptalking occurs during stage 2 sleep; REM sleeptalking is rare. Sleeptalking usually bears no relation to the sleeper's environment or (as far as anyone can tell) to the content of a dream. Treatment is rarely needed or prescribed, unless sleep-related epileptic seizures are suspected. When sleeptalking occurs in combination with sleepwalking, doctors sometimes recommend medication.

I grind my teeth in my sleep. Is that serious?

If you wake up with sore jaw muscles or your dentist observes damage to your teeth, you may suffer from bruxism, or the grinding, clenching, or clicking of the teeth during sleep. As many as one in five of us is a teeth grinder, but it is most common in the preteen and teen years. Stress may bring it on or worsen it. The treatment is a mouth guard fitted by a dentist and worn during sleep.

What is sleeping sickness?

Sleeping sickness is a common name that describes several different diseases, none of them a disorder of sleep. One form is the viral disease called lethargic (or endemic) encephalitis. (Encephalitis means "inflammation of the brain.") Its symptoms include apa-

The tsetse fly *Glossina* carries the parasite that causes sleeping sickness.

thy, drowsiness, muscle weakness, paralysis of eye muscles, and impaired vision. An epidemic of that disease swept the world between 1915 and 1926.

Today, the term more often refers to either of two forms of African trypanosomiasis. These are not disorders of sleep, although drowsiness during the day and insomnia at night are among their symptoms. They are infections caused by the microorganism of the genus *Trypanosoma*. Trypanosomes are microscopic, single-celled, and animal-like. They move by whipping their long, slender flagella. The trypanosomes travel in the blood of the tsetse fly. When the trypanosome enters the blood of a human or other animal, it attacks first the lymphatic system, then the central nervous system. Symptoms include fever, headache, and weakness followed by confusion, coma, and death. The disease is common in tropical Africa where the tsetse fly lives. African trypanosomiasis is estimated to infect between three hundred thousand and five hundred thousand Africans, most in the sub-Saharan regions of the continent. The disease is almost always fatal if not treated with medication.

Can lack of sleep kill?

Yes, but not in the way you may think. No human has ever died from being kept awake or from voluntarily staying awake. The pressure to sleep is too great, and it forces sleep long before sleep deprivation can become life-threatening. However, sleeplessness can kill gradually. In laboratory experiments, rats have been deprived of sleep, shortening their normal life span of two to three years to two weeks. What exactly kills them remains a mystery. They eat more but lose weight, and their body temperature declines steadily. Brain cells do not degenerate or die. Some brain areas may, however, produce less protein and perhaps lower levels of hormones that affect brain functions. Whatever the cause of death is, it can be prevented. If allowed to sleep near the end of their second week awake, most of the rats appeared to recover fully.

In humans, the rare disorder fatal familial insomnia (FFI) kills after six to thirty months of sleeplessness. It is an inherited disease caused by a mutation in a protein in the brain. Without sleep, the sufferer develops high blood pressure and fever. The thalamus in the brain degenerates, and the body's hormonal regulators go out of control. Weight loss, tremors, and semiconsciousness are followed by death when many organs and organ systems fail. The disease is so rare, only sixty cases in twenty-eight families have been diagnosed worldwide since 1986.

FFI is extremely rare, but other deaths caused by sleep loss are not. These are the deaths that result from accidents when drowsy drivers fall asleep at the wheel or when fatigued workers make mistakes in handling power tools and heavy equipment. These are the deaths that are preventable. "It is obvious that we can and do cheat on the amount of sleep we have to accommodate to technological and societal demands," writes Stanley Coren in *Sleep Thieves*. "Unfortunately," he adds, "such cheating can ultimately make us clumsy, stupid, unhappy, and dead."

One Night in a Sleep Lab

by Steven R. Wills

· · · · ·

I have been one acquainted with the night.

ROBERT FROST

· · · · ·

Mark is a real estate agent. His hobbies are computers and theater. At age fifty-eight, he is carrying more than a little extra weight, he admits shyly, and his medical history includes both a heart condition and a bout of depression. Recently, Mark saw a sleep specialist because he was feeling tired during the day and tossing and turning at night. His wife complained of his snoring. Mark's doctor, who was both a neurologist and a board-certified sleep specialist, listened to Mark's complaints and recommended a night in a sleep lab. "We'll monitor your sleep and find out what's going on," she said, "but first we'll check

you out here." She listened to Mark's heart and lungs, tested his reflexes, and sent a sample of his blood to the lab for testing. All results came back normal, so his "sleep study" was scheduled.

Mark describes his experience at the sleep lab:

They told me to come to the sleep clinic at 9 P.M. and when it's your turn, they wire you up. [Some thirty to thirty-five separate electrodes were attached to Mark's body to record various life signs.] After they attach the dime-sized sensors to your body, they attach all the wires to a central unit strapped around your waist. Then

· 124 ·

you're free to watch TV or do your normal evening thing until you're ready to go to bed. When you tell them [you're ready to go to sleep], they come in and secure the electrodes to their recording equipment. There is a camera to watch [you sleep] and the lights are out; so I'm sure they used infrared [photography], because it's a very dark environment. And so—you go to sleep! It's awkward but [the sensors and wires] didn't prevent me from sleeping. Then, you get up in the morning, and they remove all the sensors and send you home.

A sleep lab or sleep clinic like the one Mark went to gathers information that helps doctors find out whether their patients have sleep disorders, or whether treatments for sleep disorders are effective. In the sleep lab, electronic recording devices gather information about electrical activity in the brain, heart rate, blood pressure, the amount of oxygen in the blood, body movements, and much more. Although the sleep lab routine is unfamiliar and the electrodes might be uncomfortable, they rarely prevent patients from sleeping. Nearly every-one gets some shut-eye. "Our purpose," says a representative of the Stanford Sleep Disorders Clinic in Stanford, California, "is to diagnose and treat patients who have difficulties falling asleep or staying asleep at night, problems with excessive daytime sleepiness, or other medical problems that may occur or exacerbate during sleep."

The Stanford Sleep Clinic is large, but some are small. A typical clinic has a reception area and waiting area, a doctor's office, perhaps a half-dozen "bedrooms" (which may have a private bath), and a "control center." The bedrooms are small and minimally decorated, although the beds are usually more comfortable than most hospital beds. Every room has a television set and a reading lamp to help patients relax and fall asleep. A camera mounted on the ceiling uses either an infrared or an ultraviolet light source, so the patient can sleep in the dark while the camera records movements.

In the control center, each patient is monitored by a computer. In Mark's clinic, overnight technicians monitored Mark's EEG and vital signs and watched him as he

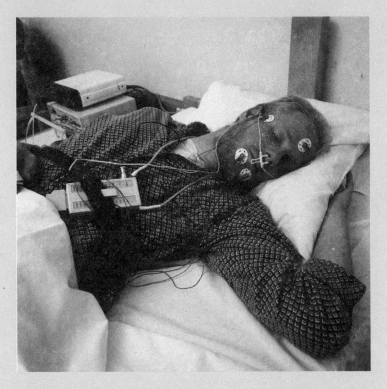

In the sleep lab, electrodes attached to the head detect electrical activity in the brain.

slept. He fell asleep with his television on, so they used their remote controls to turn it off. Mark woke and needed to go to the bathroom. The technicians went to his room and unhooked his electrodes so he could leave his bed, then hooked him up once more when he returned. After he fell asleep again, they continued their watching and recording. By morning, the technicians had gathered the equivalent of about a thousand pages of electrical information and eight hours of videotape as raw data to document Mark's stay.

Mark's doctor looked at his sleep lab recordings and diagnosed obstructive sleep apnea. It's the most common diagnosis made from sleep lab data, but it's not the only reason people go to sleep labs. Other disorders that bring people to sleep labs include insomnia, chronic fatigue, excessive daytime sleepiness, nightmares and night terrors, sleepwalking, sleeptalking, and bed-wetting. Mark's doctor explained all his test results and recommended CPAP for his sleep apnea (see page 101). It took a while for Mark to get used to sleeping with the device, but he adjusted, and now he says he is feeling much better. He says he is sleeping well and that he feels more energetic. His wife is grateful that his snoring no longer disturbs her sleep.

If you think a trip to a sleep lab might be for you, begin with your family doctor and a survey of your sleep habits. These surveys are readily available from most doctors or from hospital sleep lab websites. If you are referred to a sleep lab, make sure you find one accredited by the American Academy of Sleep Medicine. If there isn't one near you, hang on. There will be soon. In 1978, there were only three accredited sleep labs in the United States. In 2003, there were 678. More than a third of them were less than three years old. Why has the number of sleep labs grown so much? The development of technologies to monitor sleep is only part of the answer. The other part lies in how well—or how poorly!—we sleep. With three out of every four Americans experiencing some symptom of a sleep disorder a few nights a week or more, don't be surprised if the newest wing at your local hospital turns out to be a sleep laboratory.

CHAPTER FIVE

QUESTIONS

ABOUT DREAMS
AND DREAMING

*Dreaming permits each and every one of us to be quietly
and safely insane every night of our lives.*

• WILLIAM C. DEMENT •

**What's
a dream?**

Although Cinderella defined a dream as a wish the heart makes, scientists say dreams are stories our brains create while we sleep. Whether those stories have a purpose or function remains a matter of debate. Says University of California, Santa Cruz, sleep scientist Bill Domhoff, "Dreaming is the kind of freewheeling thinking that the mind goes through when there is no external input to bring it back to reality." Not all dreams are the same, and their qualities depend, at least in part, on the stage of sleep in which they occur. Dreams experienced during REM sleep tend to be bizarre and detailed. Like a movie or a novel, they have a story line. Dreams in stages 1 and 2, light sleep, are simpler and shorter than REM dreams. Deep-sleep dreams are more diffuse. They may be about nothing more than a color or an emotion.

Whatever the experience of dreaming may be, it is different from our waking experience in identifiable ways. The table below compares and contrasts the "realities" of our waking and dreaming hours by listing specific functions and showing how active each of these functions are during our dreams.

FUNCTION	DREAM COMPARED TO AWAKE
Perception of the environment	Low
Imagination	High
Attention	Lost
Recent memory	Low
Past memory	High
Emotion	Mild to intense
Reasoning and logic	Weak to absent
Information processing	Random associations
Self-reflection	Weak
Storytelling	Fanciful, freewheeling
Willpower	Weak

When do we dream?

Most dreams—and the most vivid dreams—happen during REM and sleep, but we can dream in non-REM sleep, especially late in the sleep period. When awakened from REM sleep, children under age five report dreams only about 20 to 25 percent of the time. That suggests that REM sleep does not automatically bring on dreams.

How often do we dream?

According to *First* magazine, the average person has about 1,460 dreams a year. That's four every night.

How much of our sleep time do we spend dreaming?

Estimates vary from 10 to 30 percent. So if you sleep for nine hours, you may spend as few as 54 minutes or as many as 162 minutes dreaming. At the beginning of the night, dreams are short—about twenty minutes long. They typically occur about once every ninety minutes (in REM sleep) and get longer as the night goes on.

Is vision the only "dream sense"?

No, but it's the prominent one, at least for sighted people. About half of all dreams have sounds in them, but only 1 percent have taste, smell, or touch. Nevertheless, a third of men and 40 percent of women report having experienced smell or taste in a dream at least once in their lives.

What happens in the brain during dreams?

When REM sleep begins (and dreams become more likely), an increasing number of nerve impulses rise from a region of the brain stem called the pons and nearby parts of the midbrain. The brain areas that control arousal are

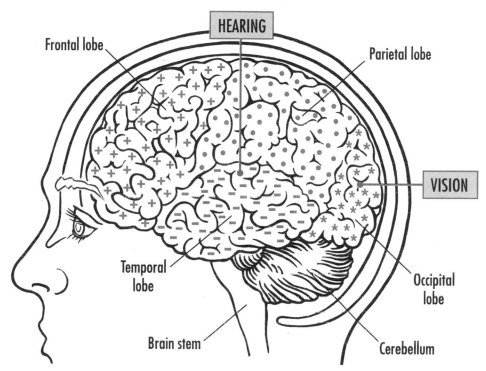

HEARING

Frontal lobe

Parietal lobe

VISION

Temporal
lobe

Occipital
lobe

Brain stem

Cerebellum

Brain regions that process sights and sounds are active during dreaming, although inputs from the eyes and ears are shut down.

more active during dreaming than during the waking hours, as are parts of the limbic system associated with emotion, motivation, and memory formation. The visual and auditory (sound processing) regions of the brain are also active during REM sleep, although the centers that process input directly from the eyes and ears are shut down. Their action may explain why we laugh and cry in our dreams, recall real people and events, "see" vivid images, and "hear" voices and sounds. The "big sleep" of dreamtime occurs in parts of the cortex that handle—during the waking hours—planning, logic, and sequential thinking. The cortex's "dozing" may explain why many dreams don't make sense and the dreaming brain doesn't care.

Although the dreams of children are often static images, most adult dreams involve objects and people that seem to move about. That's because the area of the brain's cortex that handles spatial relations when we are awake is also active during dreaming. The area also works when we practice mental imagery—such as mentally "practicing" a dive or a dance step—during the waking hours. People with injuries to either of the lower parietal lobes, where spatial information is processed, lose their ability to dream.

What's a nightmare?

Nightmares are vivid and terrifying dreams. Typically, the dreamer wakes from REM sleep, describing a detailed, frightening story. Nightmares produce enough anxiety that the person may have trouble getting back to sleep. Between 20 and 39 percent of children ages five to twelve experience nightmares. The content of nightmares is predictable from the dreamer's age. Toddlers have nightmares about separation from their parents. Preschoolers have nightmares about monsters or the dark, whereas school-age children have nightmares about death or real dangers. Adults may have nightmares about falling, being attacked, or dying. In children, nightmares may go along with sleepwalking, night terrors, or bed-wetting. Nightmares are seldom anything to worry about. In fact, they may actually help us cope with stress. For the person who feels anxious about a vivid or recurring nightmare, counseling may be helpful.

Can frightening events or scary movies cause nightmares?

After living through the great fire of London, diarist Samuel Pepys wrote in 1667, "To this very day I cannot sleep a night without great terrors of the fire." Nightmares affect soldiers when they return from combat. They also disturb the sleep of civilians who survive extreme physical or emotional traumas. Nightmares following some traumatic event can occur during stage 2 sleep, but the most frightening ones occur during REM. Violent TV shows or movies can trigger nightmares, and the University of Michigan Pediatric Advisor service warns parents against them:

> For many children, violent shows or horror movies cause bedtime fears and nightmares. These fears can persist for months or years. Absolutely forbid these movies before 13 years of age. Between 13 and 17 years, the maturity and sensitivity of your child must be considered carefully in deciding when he is ready to deal with the uncut versions of R-rated movies. Be vigilant about slumber parties or Halloween parties. Tell your child to call you if the family he or she is visiting is showing scary movies.

The service advises parents to call their health care provider when nightmares worsen, the child has several fears, or nightmares interfere with normal daytime activities.

What are night terrors?

Night terrors are not the same as nightmares. They are episodes of extreme panic that usually occur early in the sleep period. They affect perhaps 1 to 4 percent of children between the ages of four and twelve. The child does not wake but may sit up in bed and scream with what looks to parents like intense fear. Electroencephalograms (EEGs) show that the central nervous system (neurons of the brain and spinal cord) is aroused during a night terror event, which typically occurs during stage 3 or 4 of the first sleep cycle. The child's eyes are open, but the child is still asleep and does not remember the night terrors the next morning. Children typically grow out of their night terrors and experience no long-term ill effects.

Night terrors are rare in adults. They most often occur in those who abuse drugs or alcohol or who have some other sleep disorder, such as sleep apnea.

Why don't we remember our dreams?

One theory suggests that, because the neurons in the brain's cortex that control the initial storage of new memories are turned off during sleep, we forget our dreams on awaking. But because people can train themselves to remember their dreams, some experts think it's a matter of motivation and attention. Either way, it's probably good that we don't remember most of our dreams. Life would be confusing indeed if we could not distinguish dreams from real-life memories.

Why do we dream?

No one knows, but there's no shortage of theories:

- Dreams have no reason or purpose. They are chance events.

- Dreams reveal wishes or desires we are not aware of during waking hours.
- The human brain contains a vast store of information, memories, and emotion. During sleep, nerve cells fire at random, throwing bits of all of them together in random, bizarre ways.
- Dreams are a way of "taking out the trash." They allow us to process, sort, and "clean up" the emotions and experiences of the waking hours.
- Dreams are a way of solving problems creatively. We see connections and solutions during sleep that we don't perceive during waking hours.
- Dreams are an individual's "strategy for survival." During dreams, we store the information needed to recognize and deal with threats.

One of the most popular theories today is that dreaming—specifically dreaming during REM sleep—is essential for making memories. Several observations support that hypothesis. For one, when learning a new skill, REM sleep episodes are more frequent and last longer. When the new skill is mastered, those measures drop back to the normal average. Also, during REM sleep, areas in the brain's memory-forming regions appear to "replay" patterns of nerve firing associated with the new learning. Whether this has anything to do with dreaming is unknown.

Also unknown is how memories of recent events stored in the brain's hippocampus are transferred to the cortex for long-term storage. Brain imaging studies suggest this process may occur during non-REM sleep. During REM, the process may be reversed. It's possible that information "flows" back from the cortex to the hippocampus, which may explain why long-forgotten people and events pop up in dreams.

Another popular theory is that dreaming helps us regulate emotions and solve life's problems. For example, a study of women going through difficult divorces showed that their dreams predicted how well they coped with the change in their lives. Those who dreamed of the ex-spouse in a casual or distant manner recovered relatively quickly and coped well with their life change. "The preliminary data suggest that emotional problem solving takes place during dreaming," says researcher Rosalind Cartwright.

Do dreams have meaning?

The founder of psychoanalysis, Sigmund Freud (1856–1939), called dreams "the royal road to a knowledge of the unconscious mind." Dreams are messages to ourselves that we don't hear when we are awake, he claimed. In his classic book *The Interpretation of Dreams*, first published in 1900, Freud said that a dream is a story told in symbols, something like a parable or a fable. The dreamer's hidden wishes play out in disguise. For example, a bird in flight may represent a desire to travel for one dreamer. For another, it may symbolize a repressed wish to escape an unpleasant life situation. Dreams may be attempts of the unconscious to understand and overcome threatening or hurtful experiences, Freud said.

Freud thought that the dreamer's anxieties, unconscious motives, and suppressed desires surfaced in dreams. Modern techniques that take "snapshots" of the living brain in action suggest he may have been at least partly right. Brain imaging pictures show that the brain regions in charge of emotions and visual imagery are highly active during REM sleep. So are the areas associated with motivation, goals, cravings, and memory. People who have suffered injuries to those areas cease to care about their lives. They lose their ambition, imagi-

Sigmund Freud, the father of psychoanalysis, believed that dreams express repressed wishes in obscure symbols.

nation, and ability to plan. They also stop dreaming.

Accepting Freud's notion that dreams reveal unconscious wishes, many therapists ask their patients to record and evaluate their dreams. Translating the language of dreams, they think, helps people understand and solve their problems. J. Allan Hobson at Harvard University disagrees. He says using modern neuroscience to support Freud's theories is "trying to pump up a flat tire." Hobson rejects the notion of symbols in dreams. He thinks dream images are just what they seem to be—images and nothing more. In his view, dreaming is an attempt of higher brain centers to make sense of random impulses arising from the brain stem.

Still other dream-reading scientists think dreams can be both random neural firings and expressions of wishes, anxieties, or motivations. While the cortex is processing signals from the brain stem, they say, the subconscious mind may be selecting and creating images that mean something to the dreamer. Dreams, then, probably aren't abstract symbols the way Freud thought of them, but dream-events may relate to waking-world variables. For example, in one study, young adults who were unhappy in their jobs dreamed about being chased more than those who were happy in their work. In another, stockbrokers reported their dreams during a week when stock prices hit a severe low. The more stressed the stockbrokers felt, the more they dreamed of being chased or falling.

In practical terms, the images in dreams are significant if the dreamer believes they are. If a dream seems important to you, it probably is. And it probably means what you think it does. Dreams don't "release" hidden desires or "uncover" repressed motives, says University of California sleep expert William Domhoff. "Dream content is continuous with waking thought and behavior," he writes.

A DREAM DICTIONARY: FANTASY BUT FUN

A dream of a full bottle forecasts prosperity. An empty bottle means a reversal of fortunes. To dream of spilling something from a bottle predicts pesky worries and quarrels with loved ones. Or so says a "dream dictionary."

Although scientists disagree about whether dreams use symbols, all agree that the symbols— if they exist at all—are unique to each dreamer. That means dream dictionaries may be great for party games, but not much help in planning your life.

Just for fun, however, try matching the dream images in the left-hand column with a dream dictionary's interpretation on the right.

1. navel (your own)	a. new and interesting friends
2. navel (someone else's)	b. travel
3. bullfrog (you see one)	c. wealth or money
4. bullfrog (you hear one)	d. a profitable new venture
5. doughnuts	e. It's party time!
6. magnifying glass	f. failure due to vanity or overconfidence
7. peacock	g. future contentment
8. sundial	h. new love

Answers: 1. d, 2. h, 3. a, 4. g, 5. b, 6. c, 7. f, 8. e

Do we dream about our daytime activities?

Rarely. Few dreams actually review the events of the day. The stories of our dreams may be set in our daily environment and feature the people we often interact with, but the story is a literal replay of an episode in only 1 to 2 percent of dream reports.

However, "the vast majority of dreams elicited in sleep labs, by waking people up right after a REM episode, deal with everyday matters," says University of California physician Jerold Lowenstein. "Lawyers dream about courtrooms, doctors dream about operating rooms, students dream about classrooms. Dreams early in the night tend to deal with present situations, whereas dreams in the morning are more likely to go back to the dreamer's early childhood." One surprising finding, Lowenstein says, is that it takes several days for a dreamer's recent experiences to be incorporated into dreams.

Should I try to remember my dreams?

There's no harm in it, and some people find it entertaining, but it is not easy. The only way to achieve it is to review the dream immediately on awakening and write down what you remember.

Some people are so interested in their dreams that they even train themselves to wake several times during the night to record their dreams in journals. Unless you relish dream journaling as a hobby, there's little point. "So, unless you find your dreams fun, intellectually interesting, or artistically inspiring, then feel free to forget your dreams," says scientist William Domhoff. "If they just upset you or leave you puzzled, then why bother with them?"

Do babies dream?

Newborns sleep a lot, typically fourteen to eighteen hours a day. Half that time is spent in REM sleep, which is the most likely dream sleep stage in older people. A baby's brain is very active at this time, but it seems unlikely that infants have the kinds of dreams that children and adults do. Instead, many experts think REM sleep in infants stimulates brain development. The fact that premature infants spend even more of their time in REM than full-term babies do suggests that might be true.

Do young children have the same dreams as adults?

Sleep researcher David Foulkes has made a career of studying children's dreams. True dreaming, he says, starts between ages seven and nine. Before that, "dreams" are probably fanciful reports of real-life experiences or fears.

In his sleep laboratory, Foulkes awakened children of different ages. Before the age of nine, children reported dreams in only 20 to 30 percent of REM awakenings, compared with 79 percent among adults. The three- to five-year-olds he interviewed usually reported no dreams at all. Occasionally, they mentioned an animal, such as a bird, or a body state, such as feeling hungry, but they didn't tell stories. The images in their dreams did not move, and Foulkes believes that very young children are unable to imagine activity.

Beginning at age five, dreams of simple events begin. People and animals move and interact, but the stories are not well developed. Children do not see themselves in their own dreams or perceive themselves as being part of a dream. Negative feelings such as aggression, misfortune, or fear are rare in children's dream reports. Their dreams are most often pleasant and involve play more than school or television.

Between ages seven and nine, young dreamers begin to become actively involved in their own dreams. The emotional content and perceived meaning are greater. Dream reports get longer and more complex. Now there is narrative, action, character, and movement involving friends, family, or pet animals. Between ages nine and twelve, children's dreams become more like those of adults.

Around ages eleven to thirteen, dreams begin to reflect the personality of the dreamer. Preteens who are active in real life are active in their dreams. Those who are passive during the day are equally passive in the fantasy world of dreaming. Troubled dreams become more common between ages thirteen and fifteen. Dreams at this age are as long as adult dreams and as complex. Older teenagers begin to observe themselves as actors in their dreams, just as adults do.

I don't dream. Am I normal?

Colorado sleep researcher Jim Pagel invited people who said they didn't dream to his sleep laboratory. He awakened them during periods of REM sleep and asked for their dream reports. As expected, they had none. He concluded that some people do not dream, although it's possible that they dream but simply cannot recall their dreams.

Are there some common dreams that nearly everyone has?

We all dream the same things, and what we dream about is remarkably resistant to the influences of time, culture, or geography. For example, the dreams of college students in the United States stayed mostly the same between 1950 and 1980, despite major cultural changes that occurred during that time. Other studies show that the content of an adult's dreams changes little over a lifetime. Older adults dream about the same things that college students do.

Dreams seldom involve current events, political situations, or world issues. As dreamers, we are self-centered. We dream about ourselves and the circumstances of our lives. We all have more or less the same dreams, although men and women differ in how often they report them, as the table shows:

TOP DREAMS BY GENDER

DREAM	Percent who have had these dreams	
	MEN	WOMEN
1. Chased or pursued, not injured	78%	83%
2. Sexual experiences	85%	73%
3. Falling	73%	74%
4. School, teachers, studying	57%	71%
5. Arriving too late, e.g., for a train	55%	62%
6. On the verge of falling	53%	60%
7. Trying to do something repeatedly	55%	53%
8. A person now living as dead	43%	59%
9. Flying or soaring through the air	58%	44%
10. Sensing a presence vividly	44%	50%
11. Failing an examination	37%	48%
12. Being physically attacked	40%	44%
13. Being frozen with fright	32%	44%
14. A person now dead as living	37%	39%
15. Being a child again	33%	38%

Although most people have sexual dreams, only about 10 percent of dreams have sexual behavior as their content, whether kissing, petting, or sexual intercourse.

TEST YOUR DREAM IQ

True or False

Most dreams are in color.	True. When awakened from REM sleep in a laboratory, two-thirds of the dream reports include color. Later, people aren't so sure. Color, like other details in dreams, is easily forgotten.
Eating spicy food brings on more dreams or bad dreams.	False. Anything that disturbs sleep and wakes the sleeper more often increases the number of dreams the sleeper is aware of, not the number actually experienced.
The eye movements of REM sleep follow the action of a dream, like watching a movie.	False . . . maybe. Some recent studies suggest this may be true, but past attempts to match eye movements to dream content have failed. Fetuses, brain-damaged cats, and people who are blind have rapid eye movements during their sleep, and they have no "moving picture" to track.
A dream of falling and hitting the ground means you are dying.	False. Many people have this dream with no ill effects.
Hypnosis is useless for getting dream reports.	True. People don't remember their dreams under hypnosis any better than they do when awake.

Can something that is really happening be incorporated into a dream? It's not uncommon for a full bladder to elicit a dream of searching for a bathroom and for a cold foot dangling outside the covers to translate into a dream of walking in snow. Tastes and odors show up in dreams, too, but we know little about how or why. Pain can be experienced in dreams, but it's rare in healthy people. Dream pain seems to go along with real-life pain. In one study, nearly 40 percent of patients in a hospital burn unit reported a pain dream at least once in a five-day period.

Still, it remains difficult to control what we dream about, and trying to suppress thoughts about particular people or events makes dreaming about them even more likely. Sleep researchers achieve mixed results when they try to influence dream content using environmental stimuli. One study using pressure cuffs to push on sleepers' legs got leg sensations into 80 percent of reported dreams. Other studies got a water spray into 42 percent of dreams and a mild electric shock into 45 percent.

How common are recurrent dreams? Between 50 and 80 percent of us have had a recurrent dream, often starting in late childhood or adolescence and lasting for the rest of our lives. The dream is usually one of misfortune, and the dreamer finds it emotionally upsetting.

What is lucid dreaming? Have you ever been dreaming and known that you were dreaming? If you have, you've had a lucid dream. Most people experience a lucid dream at least once in their lives, and 20 percent of us have lucid dreams once a month or more. The awareness of dreaming while dreaming usually occurs during REM sleep. It may be a result of greater-than-normal activity in the areas of the brain that give us our "sense of self" while awake. On EEG tracings, it shows up as higher levels of alpha-wave activity during REM, although these are usually seen only in stage 1, light sleep.

In some lucid dreams, the sleeper has some control over the events that occur. The dreamer may be able to think, plan, reason, take action, and remember much as when awake. Some sleepers have even experienced a dream of waking up, when they in truth continued to sleep. Most lucid dreamers report enjoying the experience of willing themselves to do marvelous things in their lucid dreams, like flying or passing through walls. Lucid dreaming can be so much fun that books and classes are available to help people learn to do it more frequently. In some sleep laboratory experiments, lucid dreamers have even learned to signal with hand movements when they are having lucid dreams and to indicate to observers what they are dreaming about. Although some researchers consider lucid dreaming little more than a curiosity, others think it has potential for promoting health—possibly helping people who suffer from recurrent nightmares.

Do people who are blind dream? It depends on when they lost their sight. People who are born blind have no visual images either in waking life or in their dreams. They do, however, have activity in the visual processing areas of the brain during sleep, so they may experience some "virtual images." Individuals who lost their sight before the age of five seldom experience visual imagery in their dreams, whereas those who become sightless between the ages of five and seven may.

Most people who lost their vision after age seven continue to "see" in their dreams, although the images tend to fade as they grow older. Although people who are blind report fewer visual images, they report more taste, smell, and touch sensations in their dreams. Compared with sighted people, people who are blind report more dreams about falling or encountering a misfortune while moving around—a concern they also express in their waking hours.

Do males and females have different dreams?

In studying one thousand dreams reported by both men and women, Calvin S. Hall found that male and female characters appear with equal frequency in women's dreams. Men dream about other men about twice as often. Men's dreams are more often set outdoors, are more action-oriented, and involve strangers more often than women's dreams do. Women's dreams happen indoors and involve emotional encounters with people they know and care about. Males are more likely than females to dream about aggression, misfortunate, and negative emotions such as fear, anger, anxiety, or disgust. Women's dreams are more often friendly and positive in both the events they portray and the emotions that underlie them.

What's a daydream?

When researchers asked volunteers to relax in a dark room, some 15 to 20 percent reported dreamlike stories when asked what was going through their minds. Experts think daydreams occur when stimulation from the environment and self-control are lessened and certain areas of the brain become active as they do during dream sleep.

Do Animals Dream?

. . . . .

*It is a shame that when we have a good dream
we are asleep at the time.*

P. K. SHAW

. . . . .

My dog Dave whines and twitches, his eyes darting and jerking beneath fluttering lids as he growls softly in his sleep. Is he chasing a dream rabbit? Despite Dave's silence on the subject, I'm convinced he dreams. For many years, scientists avoided the question, because they had no way to investigate it. Now, new techniques are making research into animal dreams possible.

"Some tantalizing pieces of evidence suggest that animals dream," says Ruth Propper, a psychologist at Merrimack College in North Andover, Massachusetts. The biggest clue, she says, is REM sleep. REM is most often associated with dreams in humans. Birds and nearly all mammals twitch and move while in REM sleep, and their EEGs show patterns of heightened activity in the brain. "Since this is similar to humans, we tend to think the animal might be dreaming," Propper says. Michael Noonan of Canisius College in Buffalo, New York, agrees. He thinks animals dream just as humans do. "Our brains are similar, our neurochemistry the same, and our reflexes and memory are wired in a like manner," he says.

Some of the first evidence Propper and Noonan may be right came from the work of French scientist Michel Jouvet in 1963. He worked with cats and noticed that

during REM sleep, they behave as people do. They move little, despite tossing and turning in other stages of sleep. Jouvet found that the brain sends signals to the muscles during REM sleep. The signals for jerks and growls get through, but a region of the brain stem blocks impulses to the large muscles of the arms and legs, bringing on "sleep paralysis."

Jouvet performed surgery on some of the cats. He cut the sleep paralysis pathway in the brain stem. His cats were then free to move about during REM sleep. Jouvet watched his sleeping cats do kittenish things—chasing, leaping, and pounc-ing on a ball that wasn't there! The cats stood, arched their backs, and fought—with enemies only they could see! Jouvet drew the obvious conclusion: his cats were acting out their dreams.

A decade later, J. Allan Hobson and Robert McCarley at Harvard also studied cats, but in a different way. They found that an area near the base of the brain produces strong, rhythmic bursts of nerve signals during REM sleep. The signals travel upward and spread through the cortex, the brain's thin outer layer where most of its "thinking" functions take place. These bursts from the lower brain region must be the source of dreams, Hobson and McCarley decided. The cortex, they suggested, was doing what it always does—attempting to make sense of incoming signals. The result would be the cats' dream of pouncing or chasing.

In 2001, Kenway Louie and Matthew Wilson at the Massachusetts Institute of Technology tried yet another approach, this time with rats. They trained the animals to run a track. They used electrodes to map the firing of individual neurons in the hippocampus of the animals' brains. The pattern of nerve activity in the hippocampus was similar during training and during REM sleep. The animals were replaying their training. From this replay, Wilson says, "we know that they [the animals] are in fact dreaming and that their dreams are connected to actual experiences." But why do animals replay one experience during REM sleep and not another? Wilson hopes to find out by teaching animals different tasks, then recording which ones they replay.

Despite these findings, some scientists remain skeptical about defining or observing human-style dreams in nonhuman animals. "Dreams may be a form of consciousness, and there is no consensus among scientists whether or not lower vertebrates or dogs or cats have forms of consciousness that can sustain dreams as we understand them," says neuroscientist Marcos Frank of the University of Pennsylvania School of Medicine. So even if animals dream, they probably don't make up stories of people, events, situations, and emotions the way humans do. If dogs dream at all, they probably have . . . well . . . dog dreams. If my dog Dave could talk, he could tell us about them, but so far he's stayed silent on the subject. Until he reveals his secrets, I'll continue to believe he dreams. He awakened from his nap moments ago with a self-satisfied look on his face. I think he treed a dream squirrel.

IN CLOSING

MORE QUESTIONS
THAN ANSWERS

*Come Sleep! Oh, Sleep, the certain knot of peace, the
baiting-place of wit, the balm of woe, the poor man's
wealth, the prisoner's release, the indifferent judge
between the high and low.*

• Sir Philip Sidney •

What have you thought about as you've read the questions and answers on these pages? Perhaps you have been struck by how complex an apparently simple thing like sleep actually is. Sleep is as fundamental to our survival as breathing, yet we understand only a little about it. For many centuries, sleep and dreams were the stuff of legends, myths, and campfire tales. What we could not observe, measure, or investigate we described in supernatural terms—as visits from spirits or augurs of the future. Before the 1950s, most people thought of sleep as a static (and rather boring) period of rest for the body. Then, in 1953, scientists observed and described REM sleep, and the era of modern sleep research began. Fifty years is a short time in the history of science. Sleep research is still in its infancy.

Probing the secrets of sleep is like exploring distant galaxies. We have a general idea of the terrain, but our maps are limited until we can get a closer look. With each passing year, our eyes, our instruments, and our experiments probe further beyond what we know into a world we can only imagine. The frontiers of space exploration are distant galaxies, pulsars, and supernovas only giant telescopes can pinpoint. The frontiers of sleep science are neurons, neurotransmitters, and brain scans of intricate complexity.

Sleeping and dreaming are such complicated processes, can anyone ever possibly understand them completely? The truth is, probably not. Today in laboratories all over the world, scientists are striving to unlock the secrets of sleep and dreams, and what they learn may well prolong life and promote health for generations to come. But each question answered raises more questions. No matter how far we have come in understanding sleep, we still have a long way to go. That peaceful slumber we take for granted will long remain a mystery. Sleepers, alas, can but dimly perceive their own sleep.

GLOSSARY

active sleep: a form of sleep observed in newborn babies in which limbs move and breathing is irregular; develops into the REM sleep of children and adults

adenosine: a compound thought to promote drowsiness and (as it accumulates in the brain) the increasing need to sleep

advanced sleep phase syndrome (ASPS): going to bed early and waking early. This circadian rhythm disorder is common among elderly people.

alpha waves: patterns of electrical activity seen in the relaxed state and early stages of sleep; characterized by wave patterns that cycle eighteen times a second

antibody: a protein in the blood, manufactured by the immune system, that locks onto invading microbes and marks them for destruction

antidepressant: a drug traditionally used to treat depression, a mental disorder characterized by feelings of sadness and often accompanied by sleep disturbances

beta waves: patterns of electrical activity in the waking brain recorded on the EEG; characterized by rapid brain-wave patterns that cycle between thirteen and thirty-five times a second

biological or "body" clock: the internal timing mechanisms that cause organisms to function, change, and behave in concert with days, months, seasons, or years. See also *circadian rhythm.*

brain waves: the brain's spontaneous electrical activity as recorded by an electroencephalograph

bruxism: teeth grinding or clenching of teeth during sleep

cataplexy: a temporary and sudden loss of muscle control often seen in people who have narcolepsy

cerebral cortex: the brain's thin outer layer that handles voluntary functions such as purposeful action and reasoning

chronotherapy: a systematic approach to changing sleeping and waking times designed to reset the biological clock

circadian rhythm: the repetitive cycling of regular body processes over approximately a twenty-four-hour period, coordinated by the suprachiasmatic nuclei (SCN) in the brain and regulating temperature, hormone secretions, sleep-waking, elimination of wastes, and other functions

coma: an unconscious state that does not produce the EEG brain-wave patterns of normal sleep

continuous positive airway pressure (CPAP): a treatment for sleep apnea that uses an air compressor to force air through the nose and into the airway during sleep

cortisol: a hormone produced in the adrenal gland associated with waking, alertness, and stress

delayed sleep phase syndrome (DSPS): going to bed late and waking late. This circadian rhythm disorder is common among adolescents.

delta waves: patterns of electrical activity seen in stages 3 and 4 sleep; characterized by long, slow waves that cycle four times a second

depression: a disorder of mood characterized by feelings of sadness and despair that last for more than two weeks

dream: a period of intense vivid imagery or (occasionally) other sensory impressions occurring during sleep; often associated with REM sleep

electroencephalogram (EEG): a recording of brain-wave patterns made by an electroencephalograph

excessive daytime sleepiness (EDS): difficulty staying awake during the normal wake period of the sleep-wake cycle

fatal familial insomnia (FFI): a rare inherited disease in which patients die from lack of sleep

gamma-amniobutyric acid (GABA): a major inhibiting neurotransmitter in the brain, present in the brain in large amounts during slow-wave sleep

hibernation: a period of winter inactivity, during which an animal's normal life processes go on at a reduced rate and less energy is expended

hypocretin: a neurotransmitter (also called orexin) that acts on the hypothalamus of the brain to promote wakefulness

hypothalamus: a region at the base of the brain that regulates numerous processes, including temperature regulation, food intake, and the sleep-wake cycle

insomnia: a general term for insufficient sleep resulting from difficulty falling asleep, waking too early and not being able to get back to sleep, waking frequently, or waking feeling tired

jet lag: a disruption of circadian rhythms associated with rapid travel across several time zones. Symptoms include fatigue, nausea, constipation, irritability, and insomnia.

lark: a "morning person," who prefers to rise early and feels most alert in the morning hours

latency: the time interval between going to bed and going to sleep

leptin: a hormone secreted by fat cells that partially regulates appetite and eating behavior

long-term potentiation (LTP): the process by which signals between neurons become strengthened and (therefore) learning occurs and memories form

lucid dream: a dream in which the sleeper is aware of dreaming

melatonin: a sleep-promoting hormone secreted by the pineal gland in the brain in response to darkness

narcolepsy: a sleep disorder characterized by episodes of inappropriate, involuntary, and sudden sleep

neuron: a nerve cell

neurotransmitter: a chemical released from the end of one neuron that transmits or blocks a nerve impulse to another neuron by binding to receptor sites on the receiving nerve cell. Neurotransmitters associated with sleep and wakefulness include norepinephrine, serotonin, acetylcholine, dopamine, adrenaline, and histamine.

nightmare: a disturbing or frightening dream, usually one that wakes the sleeper from REM sleep

night terrors: sudden partial arousals from non-REM sleep characterized by screaming and intense fear that is not consciously perceived at the time or remembered later

non-REM sleep: a general term that includes sleep stages 1 through 4

orexin: see *hypocretin*

owl: a "night person," who prefers to stay up late at night and feels most energetic in the evening or late-night hours

periodic limb movement syndrome (PLMS): a condition in which the legs or arms twitch or move involuntarily and periodically during sleep

quiet sleep: a form of non-REM sleep in infants

REM behavior disorder (RBD): a sleep disorder in which the paralysis of major muscles during REM fails, and the sleeper kicks, punches, or acts out dreams

REM sleep: also known as "paradoxical" sleep, this stage of sleep is characterized by rapid eye movement (REM), muscle paralysis, and irregular breathing, heart rate, and blood pressure. Most vivid dreaming takes place during REM sleep.

restless legs syndrome (RLS): a disorder characterized by twitching, creeping, or tingling sensations in the legs felt while sitting or lying down. Movement relieves the sensations.

retinal ganglionic cells (RGCs): cells in the eyes that respond to light and send signals to the SCN (the circadian clock in the brain)

serotonin: a neurotransmitter in the brain that affects mood, appetite, sleep, and many other body processes

shift work: working at times other than the usual daytime hours of 8:00 A.M. to 5:00 P.M.

sleep: a state in which an individual rests quietly either sitting or lying down and becomes (more or less) unresponsive to the environment

sleep apnea: a sleep disorder in which episodes of breathing cessation experienced during sleep deplete blood of oxygen and disrupt sleep

sleep cycle: the cycle in which non-REM and REM sleep alternate in approximately ninety-minute periods throughout an adult's typical night's sleep

sleep debt: a buildup of the need to sleep induced by sleep deprivation

sleep deprivation: a deficiency of sleep induced by any cause

sleep disorder: any of seventy known diseases or conditions that result in loss of sleep, abnormal sleep, or disruption of normal circadian rhythms

sleep efficiency: the fraction of time in bed that is actually spent sleeping

sleeping sickness: a general term for any of several inflammatory or infectious diseases that are not sleep disorders but may have increased sleep as a symptom

sleep paralysis: a feeling of being immobilized in bed, unable to call for help, resulting from awareness of the normal paralysis of the voluntary muscles that prevents sleepers from moving during REM sleep

sleep-wake cycle: sleep alternating with wakefulness in a twenty-four-hour period

sleepwalking: walking or performing other complicated activities while asleep and unaware

slow-wave sleep: the deep sleep of stages 3 and 4

snoring: the noise made by the vibrations of the soft palate and the uvula while breathing during sleep

soft palate: the tissues on the roof of the mouth at the back, near the throat

suprachiasmatic nucleus (SCN): a part of the brain in the hypothalamus that coordinates circadian rhythms with environmental light/dark cycles

thalamus: the area of the brain that relays sensory information to the cerebral cortex

tuberomammillary nucleus (TMN): a part of the brain (in the hypothalamus) that, when active, promotes wakefulness

uvula: the soft strip of tissue that hangs down in the back of the mouth at the opening into the throat

ventrolateral preoptic nucleus (VLPO): a region of the brain in the hypothalamus that initiates and maintains sleep

wakefulness: the brain activity and physiological processes of an individual who is not asleep

FOR FURTHER
INFORMATION

Books

Caldwell, J. Paul. *Sleep: The Complete Guide to Sleep Disorders and a Better Night's Sleep.* Rev. Ed. Buffalo, NY: Firefly Books, 2003.

Dement, William C. *The Promise of Sleep: A Pioneer in Sleep Medicine Explores the Vital Connection Between Health, Happiness, and a Good Night's Sleep.* New York: Delacorte Press, 1999.

Hauri, Peter, and Shirley Linde. *No More Sleepless Nights: A Proven Program to Conquer Insomnia.* New York: John Wiley, 1996.

Hobson, J. Allan. *Dreaming: An Introduction to the Science of Sleep.* New York: Oxford University Press, 2002.

Jouvet, Michel. *The Paradox of Sleep: The Story of Dreaming.* Cambridge, MA: MIT Press, 2001.

Kryger, Meir H. *A Woman's Guide to Sleep Disorders.* New York: McGraw-Hill, 2004.

LaBerge, Stephen, and Howard Rheingold. *Exploring the World of Lucid Dreaming.* New York: Ballantine, 1990.

Lavie, Peretz. *The Enchanted World of Sleep.* New Haven, CT: Yale University Press, 1998.

Lavie, Peretz. *Restless Nights: Understanding Snoring and Sleep Apnea.* New Haven, CT: Yale University Press, 2003.

Martin, Paul. *Counting Sheep: The Science and Pleasures of Sleep and Dreams.* London: HarperCollins, 2002.

Palmer, John D. *The Living Clock.* New York: Oxford University Press, 2002.

Rock, Andrea. *The Mind at Night: The New Science of How and Why We Dream.* Cambridge, MA: Basic Books, 2004.

Van de Castle, Robert L. *Our Dreaming Mind.* New York: Ballantine, 1994.

Walsleben, Joyce. *A Woman's Guide to Sleep.* New York: Random House, 2000.

Wilson, Virginia N. *Sleep Thief, Restless Legs Syndrome.* Orange Park, FL: Galaxy Books, 1996.

Articles

Bower, Bruce. "Brains in Dreamland." *Science News* (August 11, 2001), p. 90.

Bower, Bruce. "Slumber's Unexplored Landscape." *Science News* (September 25, 1999), p. 205.

Boyce, Neil, and Susan Brink. "The Secrets of Sleep." *U.S. News & World Report* (May 17, 2004), pp. 58–68.

Brink, Susan. "Sleepless Society." *U.S. News & World Report* (October 16, 2000), pp. 63–66ff.

Brown, Chip. "The Man Who Mistook His Wife for a Deer and Other Tales from the New Science of Extreme Sleep." *New York Times Magazine* (February 2, 2003), pp. 34ff.

Christensen, Damaris. "Is Snoring a DiZZZease?" *Science News* (March 11, 2000), pp. 172–173.

Cobb, Kristin. "Missed ZZZ's, More Disease?" *Science News* (September 7, 2002), p. 152.

Gorman, Christine. "Why We Sleep." *Time* (December 20, 2004), pp. 46–52ff.

Kantrowitz, Barbara. "In Search of Sleep." *Newsweek* (July 15, 2002), pp. 39-47.

Kantrowitz, Barbara, and Karen Springen. "What Dreams Are Made Of." *Newsweek* (August 9, 2004), pp. 40–47.

Kramer, Milton. "Dreamspeak." *Psychology Today* (September/October 2000), pp. 56–60ff.

Neimark, Jill. "Night Life." *Psychology Today* (July–August 1998), pp. 30ff.

Odyssey magazine. The January 2002 issue was devoted to sleep and dreams.

Siegel, Jerome M. "Why We Sleep." *Scientific American* (November 2003), pp. 92–97.

Winson, Jonathan. "The Meaning of Dreams." *Scientific American: Special Edition "The Hidden Mind"* (August 31, 2002), pp. 54–61.

Wright, Karen. "Times of Our Lives." *Scientific American* (September 2002), pp. 58–65.

Websites

The Apnea Patient's News, Education & Awareness Network
<www.apneanet.org>

"Brain Basics: Understanding Sleep" from the National Institute of Neurological Disorders and Stroke
<www.ninds.nih.gov/disorders/brain_basics/understanding_sleep_brain_basic.htm>

"Common Sleep Problems" at TeensHealth
<http://kidshealth.org/teen/your_body/take_care/sleep.html>

Sign up for New Abstracts and Papers in Sleep (NAPS) to keep up with the latest research at Sleep Home Pages

"What is Sleep . . . and Why Do We Do It?" from the Neuroscience for Kids project at the University of Washington
<http://faculty.washington.edu/chudler/sleep.html>

Agencies and Organizations

AAA Foundation for Traffic Safety
607 Fourteenth Street NW, Suite 201
Washington, DC 20005
<www.aaafoundation.org>
Publishes research reports on drowsy driving

American Academy of Sleep Medicine
One Westbrook Corporate Center, Suite 920
Westchester, IL 60154
<www.aasmnet.org>
Publishes fact sheets for patients and promotes sleep research

American Insomnia Association
One Westbrook Corporate Center, Suite 920
Westchester, IL 60154
<www.americaninsomniaassociation.org>
A patient-based organization that assists people who suffer from insomnia

American Sleep Apnea Association
1424 K Street NW, Suite 302
Washington, DC 20005
<www.sleepapnea.org>
Publishes a newsletter, *WAKE-UP CALL: The Wellness Letter for Snoring and Apnea*

International Association for the Study of Dreaming
1672 University Avenue
Berkeley, CA 94703
<www.asdreams.org>
Holds conferences and publishes the magazine *Dream Time*

Narcolepsy Network, Inc.
10921 Reed Hartman Highway, Suite 119
Cincinnati, OH 45242

Provides educational materials and supports research on narcolepsy

National Center on Sleep Disorders Research, National Institutes of Health
Two Rockledge Centre, Suite 7024
6701 Rockledge Drive, MSC 7920
Bethesda, MD 20892
<www.nhlbi.nih.gov/about/ncsdr>
Publishes pamphlets on narcolepsy, insomnia, and sleep apnea

National Highway Traffic Safety Administration
U.S. Department of Transportation
NHTSA Information
400 Seventh Street SW
Washington, DC 20590
<www.nhtsa.dot.gov>
Publishes pamphlets on driver fatigue and highway accidents

National Sleep Foundation
1522 K Street NW, Suite 500
Washington, DC 20005
<www.sleepfoundation.org>
Sponsors a national "Sleep awareness week" annually

Parents Against Tired Truckers
PO Box 14380
Washington, DC 20044-4380
<www.patt.org>
Publishes a newsletter, *The Truck Safety Advocate*

Restless Legs Syndrome Foundation
819 Second Street SW
Rochester, MN 55902
<www.rls.org>
Publishes a quarterly newsletter, *Night Walkers*

Society for Neuroscience
11 Dupont Circle NW, Suite 500
Washington, DC 20036
<www.sfn.org>
The society's *Brain Briefings* are available on the website.

NOTES

p. 14 Adam Zeman, "Consciousness," *Brain* (July 2001), 1263–1289.

p. 14 Ibid.

p. 16 Quoted in William J. Cromie, "Awakening to How We Sleep," *Harvard University Gazette,* March 5, 1998.

p. 16 Quoted in Usha Lee McFarling, "Even Fruit Flies Catch Their Zs," *Los Angeles Times,* January 4, 2001.

p. 19 William C. Dement and Christopher Vaughan, *The Promise of Sleep* (New York: Delacorte, 1999), 254.

p. 20 Milton Kramer, "Dreamspeak," *Psychology Today* (September–October 2000), 56–60.

p. 20 J. M. Krueger, J. A. Majde, and F. Obal Jr., "Sleep in Host Defense," *Brain, Behavior, and Immunity* (February 15, 2003), 41–47.

p. 20 L. Marshall and J. Born, "Brain-Immune Interactions in Sleep," *International Review of Neurobiology* (2002), 93–131.

p. 20 J. Savard, L. Laroche, S. Simard, et al. "Chronic Insomnia and Immune Functioning," *Psychosomatic Medicine* (March/April 2003), 211–221.

p. 21 E. Van Cauter, F. Latta, A. Nedeltcheva, et al. "Reciprocal Interactions Between the CH Axis and Sleep," *Growth Hormone & IGF Research* (June 2004, supplement A), S10–17.

p. 21 The main source for this answer is M. A. Carno, L. A. Hoffman, J. A. Carcillo, and M. H. Sanders, "Developmental Stages of Sleep from Birth to Adolescence, Common Childhood Sleep Disorders: Overview and Nursing Implications," *Journal of Pediatric Nursing* (August 2003), 274–283.

p. 22 New Abstracts and Papers in Sleep, E-mail Alert, September 10, 2001.

p. 25 Marcos G. Frank, Naoum P. Issa, and Michael P. Stryker, "Sleep Enhances Plasticity in the Developing Visual Cortex," *Neuron* (April 2001), 275–287.

p. 25 "Sleep In Early Life May Play Crucial Role in Brain Development," press release from the University of California, San Francisco, May 3, 2001.

p. 25 K. Crowley, J. Trinder, Y. Kim, et al., "The Effects of Normal Aging on Sleep Spindle and K-complex Production," *Clinical Neurophysiology* (October 2002), 1615–1622.

p. 26 E. B. Klerman, J. B. Davis, J. F. Duffy, et al., "Older People Awaken More Frequently But Fall Back Asleep at the Same Rate as Younger People," *Sleep* (June 15, 2004), 793–798.

p. 26 Judith. A. Floyd, "Sleep and Aging," *The Nursing Clinics of North America* (December 2002), 719–731.

p. 26 A. Nicolas, D. Petit, R. Rompre, and J. Montplaisir, "Sleep Spindle Characteristics in Healthy Subjects of Different Age Groups," *Clinical Neurophysiology* (March 2001), 521–527.

p. 27 Karine Spiegel, Rachel Leproult, and Eve Van Cauter, "Impact of Sleep Debt on Metabolic and Endocrine Function," *The Lancet* (October 23, 1999), 1435–1439.

p. 28 Zeman, p. 1267.

p. 28 L. C. Parsons and L. J. Crosby, "Do Comatose Patients Sleep?" *Sleep Medicine Alert* (National Sleep Foundation) 3(1): available on-line at <http://www.sleepfoundation.org/publications/sma3.1.cfm>.

p. 29 F. Giganti, M. J. Hayes, M. R. Akilesh, and P. Salzarulo, "Yawning and Behavioral States in Premature Infants," *Developmental Psychobiology* (November 2002), 289–296.

p. 29 R. R. Provine, "Yawning: Effects of Stimulus Interest," *Bulletin of the Psychonomic Society* (vol. 27, 1989), 125–126.

p. 29 Rebecca Raphael, "Is Yawning Contagious?" ABC News, February 28, 2001, available on-line at <http://abcnews.go.com>.

p. 29 R. R. Provine, "Contagious Yawning and Laughter: Significance for Sensory Feature Detection, Motor Pattern Generation, Imitation, and the Evolution of Social Behavior," in C. M. Heyes and B. G. Galef, eds., *Social Learning in Animals: The Roots of Culture* (New York: Academic Press, 1996), 179–208.

p. 30 "Steven M. Platek, S. R. Critton, T. E. Myers, and G. G. Gallup Jr., "Contagious Yawning: The Role of Self-Awareness and Mental State Attribution," *Cognitive Brain Research* (July 15, 2003), 223–227.

p. 31 " Sleep Position Gives Personality Clue," BBC News, September 16, 2003, available on-line at <http://news.bbc.co.uk/2/hi/health/3112170.stm>.

p. 33 T. Tamura, S. Miyasako, M. Ogawa, et al., "Assessment of Bed Temperature Monitoring for Detecting Body Movement During Sleep: Comparison with Simultaneous Video Image Recording and Actigraphy," *Medical Engineering & Physics* (February 1999), 1–8.

p. 33 Dana MacKenzie, "Half-Brained Ducks in a Row," *ScienceNOW*, February 3, 1999.

p. 35 Kennda Zoffka, "Sleeping with the Bears," *Odyssey* (January 2002), 38–39.

p. 35 J. E. Larkin and H. C. Heller, "The Disappearing Slow Wave Activity of Hibernators," *Sleep Research Online* (1[2], 1998), 96–101.

p. 37 O. I. Lyamin, L. M. Mukhametov, I. S. Chetybrok, and A. V. Vassiliev, "Sleep and Wakefulness in the Southern Sea Lion," *Behavioral Brain Research* (January 22, 2002), 129–138.

p. 37 Trudee Romanek, *ZZZ: The Most Interesting Book You'll Ever Read about Sleep* (Toronto: Kids Can Press, 2002), 18.

p. 37 J. M. Siegel, "Phylogenetic Data Bearing on the REM Sleep Learning Connection," *Behavioral and Brain Sciences* (December 2000), 1007.

p. 38 J. M. Siegel, P. Manger, R. Nienhuis, et al., "The Echidna Tachyglossus aculeatus Combines REM and Non-REM Aspects in a Single Sleep State: Implications for the Evolution of Sleep," *Journal of Neuroscience* (May 15, 1996), 3500–3506; and J. M Siegel, P. Manger, R. Nienhuis, et al., "Monotremes and the Evolution of Rapid Eye Movement Sleep," *Philosophical Transactions of the Royal Society: London BioScience* (July 29, 1998), 1147–1157.

p. 38 Susan Milius, "Sparrows Cheat on Sleep," *Science News* (July 17, 2004), 38.

p. 38 F. Ramon, J. Hernandez-Falcon, B. Nguyen, and T. H. Bullock, "Slow Wave Sleep in Crayfish," *Proceedings of the National Academy of Sciences of the United States of America* (July 30, 2004), available on-line at <www.pnas.org>.

p. 39 S. Sauer, M. Kinkelin, E. Hermann, and W. Kaiser, "The Dynamics of Sleep-Like Behaviour in Honeybees," *Journal of Comparative Physiology: Sensory, Neural, and Behavioral Physiology* (August 2003), 599–607.

p. 39 Paul J. Shaw, Chiara Cirelli, Ralph J. Greenspan, and Giulio Tononi, "Correlates of Sleep and Waking in Drosophila melanogaster," *Science* (March 10, 2000), 1834–1837.

p. 39 J. M. Siegel, "Sleep," Encarta.

p. 42 D. Katzenberg, T. Young, L. Finn, et al., "A CLOCK Polymorphism Associated with Human Diurnal Preference," *Sleep* (September 15, 1998), 569–576.

p. 42 Stanley Coren, "Sleep Deprivation, Psychosis and Mental Efficiency," *Psychiatric Times* (March 1998).

p. 42 "2002 'Sleep in America' Poll," National Sleep Foundation, available on-line at <www .sleepfoundation.org>.

p. 42 Op. cit.

p. 43 B. B. Kamdar, K. A. Kaplan, E. J. Kezirian, and W. C. Dement, "The Impact of Extended Sleep on Daytime Alertness, Vigilance, and Mood," *Sleep Medicine* (September 2004), 441–448.

p. 43 Gregory Belenky, "Sleep, Sleep Deprivation, and Human Performance in Continuous Operations," Division of Neuropsychiatry, Walter Reed Army Institute of Research, 1997, available on-line at <http://www.usafa.af.mil/jscope/JSCOPE97/Belenky97/Belenky97.htm>.

p. 44 Ronald E. Dahl, "The Consequences of Insufficient Sleep for Adolescents: Links Between Sleep and Emotional Regulation," *Phi Delta Kappan* (January 1999), 354–359.

p. 45 M. A. Carskadon and W. C. Dement, "Effects of Total Sleep Loss on Sleep Tendency," *Perceptual Motor Skills* (April 1979), 495–506.

p. 45 M. Engle-Friedman, S. Riela, R. Golan, et al., "The Effect of Sleep Loss on Next Day Effort," *Journal of Sleep Research* (June 2003), 113–124.

p. 46 Dahl.

p. 46 S.P.A. Drummond, G. G. Brown, J. C. Gillin, et al., "Altered Brain Response to Verbal Learning Following Sleep Deprivation," *Nature* (February 10, 2000), 655.

p. 46 Drummond, personal communication.

p. 47 M. Irwin, J. McClintick, J. Costlow, et al., "Partial Night Sleep Deprivation Reduces Natural Killer and Cellular Immune Responses in Humans," *The FASEB Journal* (April 1996), 643–653.

p. 47 "Sleep Deprivation Alters Hormonal Activity," press release, Reuters Health, June 24, 2002.

p. 48 K. Spiegel, J. F. Sheridan, and E. Van Cauter, "Effect of Sleep Deprivation on Response to Immunization," *Journal of the American Medical Association* (September 25, 2002), 1471–1472.

p. 48 T. Lange, B. Perras, H. L. Fehmn, and J. Born, "Sleep Enhances the Human Antibody Response to Hepatitis Vaccination," *Psychosomatic Medicine* (September-October 2003), 831–835.

p. 49 D. Aeshbach, C. Cajochen, H. Landolt, and A. A. Borbely, "Homeostatic Sleep Regulation in Habitual Short Sleepers and Long Sleepers," *American Journal of Physiology: Regulatory, Integrative, and Comparative Physiology* (January 1996), R41–R53.

p. 49 D. Aeschbach, L. Sher, T. T. Postolache, et al., "A Longer Biological Night in Long Sleepers Than in Short Sleepers," *The Journal of Clinical Endocrinology & Metabolism* (January 2003), 26–30.

p. 50 T. H. Monk, D. J. Buysse, D. K. Welsh, et al., "A Sleep Diary and Questionnaire Study of Naturally Short Sleepers," *Journal of Sleep Research* (September 2001), 173–179.

p. 51 William E. Kelly, "Worry and Sleep Length Revisited: Worry, Sleep Length, and Sleep Disturbance Ascribed to Worry," *The Journal of Genetic Psychology* (September 2002), 296–304.

p. 51 Michele Ferrara and Luigi De Gennaro, "How Much Sleep Do We Need?" *Sleep Medicine Reviews* (April 2001), 155–179.

p. 51 Aeschbach et al. (2003).

p. 51 Kelly.

p. 51 T. Akerstedt, P. Fredlund, M. Gillberg, and B. Jansson, "Work Load and Work Hours in Relation to Disturbed Sleep and Fatigue in a Large Representative Sample," *Journal of Psychosomatic Research* (July 2002), 585–588.

p. 52 "Sleep Debts Accrue When Nightly Sleep Totals Six Hours or Fewer," press release, University of Pennsylvania Medical Center, March 13, 2002.

p. 52 "Stanford Researchers Identify Best Hours for Shut-Eye When Sleep Must Be Limited," press release, Stanford University Medical Center, May 29, 2003.

p. 53 Rod Usher, "Reaping the Rewards of Sleep," *Time* (April 5, 1999), 83.

p. 54 K. Spiegel, R. Leproult, M. L'Hermite-Balériaux, et al., "Leptin Levels Are Dependent on Sleep Duration: Relationships with Sympathovagal Balance, Carbohydrate Regulation, Cortisol, and Thyrotropin," *Journal of Clinical Endocrinology and Metabolism* (November 2004), 5762–5771.

p. 54 G. Hasler, D. J. Buysee, R. Klaghoffer, et al., "The Association Between Short Sleep Duration and Obesity in Young Adults: A 13-year Prospective Study," *Sleep* (June 15, 2004), 661–666.

p. 54 N. K. Gupta, W. H. Mueller, W. Chan, and J. C. Meininger, "Is Obesity Associated with Poor Sleep Quality in Adolescents?" *American Journal of Human Biology* (November–December 2002), 762–768.

p. 54 M. Sekine, T. Yamagami, K. Handa, et al., "A Dose-Response Relationship Between Short Sleeping Hours and Childhood Obesity: Results of the Toyama Birth Cohort Study," *Child Care Health Development* (March 2002), 163–170.

p. 54 J. Vioque, A. Torres, and J. Quiles, "Time Spent Watching Television, Sleep Duration and Obesity in Adults Living in Valencia, Spain," *International Journal of Obesity Related Metabolic Disorders* (December 2000), 1683–1688.

p. 55 R. D. Vorona, M. P. Winn, T. W. Babineau, et. al., "Overweight and Obese Patients in a Primary Care Population Report Less Sleep Than Patients With a Normal Body Mass Index," *Archives of Internal Medicine* (January 10, 2005), 25–30.

p. 55 T. Kawada, "Changes in Rapid Eye Movement (REM) Sleep in Response to Exposure to All-Night Noise and Transient Noise," *Archives of Environmental Health* (September–October 1999), 336–340.

p. 55 A. Shourie, "In the Workplace: Time for Sleep?" *Occupational Health Tracker* (Spring 2002), 15–18.

p. 55 S. Rajaratnam and J. Arendt, "Health in a 24-Hour Society," *The Lancet* (September 22, 2001) 358: 999–1005.

p. 56 Op. cit.

p. 56 M. B. Weinger and S. Ancoli-Israel, "Sleep Deprivation and Clinical Performance," *Journal of the American Medical Association* (February 27, 2002), 955–957.

p. 56 D. J. Shroeder et al., *Some Effects of 8- vs. 10-Hour Work Schedules on the Test Performance/Alertness of Air Traffic Control Specialists* (Washington, DC: Federal Aviation Administration, 1995).

p. 56 Rajaratnam and Arendt.

p. 57 William C. Dement, in the preface to D. F. Dinges and R. J. Broughton (Eds.), *Sleeping and Alertness: Chronobiological, Behavioral, and Medical Aspects of Napping* (New York: Raven Press, 1989).

p. 57 Sara C. Mednick, Ken Nakayama, Jose L. Cantero, et al., "The Restorative Effect of Naps on Perceptual Deterioration," *Nature Neuroscience* (July 2002), 677–681.

p. 58 "Afternoon Naps Improve Driver Performance," *AAA Foundation for Traffic Safety: Progress Report* (January–February 1999), 3–4.

p. 58 Op. cit. See also S. Mednick, N. Pathak, K. Nakayama, and R. Stickgold, "Perceptual Deterioration Predicts Performance Today," *Journal of Vision* (November 20, 2002), 66a.

p. 58 "'Power Nap' Prevents Burnout: Morning Sleep Perfects a Skill," *NIH News Release* (Tuesday, July 2, 2002).

p. 58 Quoted in Barbara Kantrowitz, "In Search of Sleep," *Newsweek* (July 15, 2002), 44–45.

p. 59 "2000 Omnibus Sleep in America Poll," National Sleep Foundation, available on-line at <www.sleepfoundation.org>.

p. 60 A. R. Wolfson and M.A. Carskadon, "Sleep Schedules and Daytime Functioning in Adolescents," *Child Development* (August 1998), 875–887.

p. 60 M. Carskadon, K. Harvey, P. Duke, et al., "Pubertal Changes in Daytime Sleepiness," *Sleep* (1980), 453–460; M. A. Carskadon, "Patterns of Sleep and Sleepiness in Adolescents," *Pediatrician* (1990), 5–12.

p. 60 R. Manber, R. R. Bootzin, C. Acebo, and M. A. Carskadon, "The Effects of Regularizing Sleep-Wake Schedules on Daytime Sleepiness," *Sleep* (June 1996), 432–441.

p. 61 Wolfson and Carskadon.

p. 61 National Sleep Foundation, *Adolescent Sleep Needs and Patterns: Research Report and Resource Guide* (National Sleep Foundation, 2000), 1.

p. 61 A. R. Wolfson and M. A. Carskadon, "Understanding Adolescents' Sleep Patterns and School Performance: A Critical Appraisal," *Sleep Medicine Reviews* (December 2003), 491–506.

p. 61 Ibid.

p. 61 T. Roenneberg, T. Kuehnle, P. P. Pramstaller, et al., "A Marker for the End of Adolescence," *Current Biology* (December 2004), R1038–1039.

p. 65 E. F. Pace-Schott and J. A. Hobson, "The Neurobiology of Sleep: Genetics, Cellular Physiology and Subcortical Networks," *Nature Reviews/Neuroscience* (August 2002), 591–605.

p. 66 S. R. Vincent, "The Ascending Reticular Activating System—From Aminergic Neurons to Nitric Oxide," *Journal of Chemical Neuroanatomy* (February 2000), 23–30.

p. 66 C. Gottesmann, "The Neurochemistry of Waking and Sleeping Mental Activity: The Disinhibition-Dopamine Hypothesis," *Psychiatry and Clinical Neurosciences* (August 2002), 345–354.

p. 66 Quoted in Steve Buist, "Why We Have to Sleep," *The Hamilton Spectator* (December 5, 2000).

p. 66 C. B. Saper, T. C. Chou, and T. E. Scammell, "The Sleep Switch: Hypothalamic Control of Sleep and Wakefulness," *Trends in Neuroscience* (December 2001), 726–731.

p. 67 W. Mignot, S. Taheri, and S. Nishino, "Sleeping with the Hypothalamus: Emerging Therapeutic Targets for Sleep Disorders," *Nature Neuroscience Supplement* (November 2002), 1071–1075.

p. 67 William J. Cromie, "Awakening to How We Sleep," *Harvard University Gazette* (March 5, 1998).

p. 67 C.B. Saper, et al., 2001.

p. 67 "Sleep Master Chemical Found," BBC News, 16 January 2003 available on-line at <http://news.bbc.co.uk/1/health/2664697.stm>.

p. 68 A. Steiger, "Sleep and the Hypothalamo-Pituitary-Adrenocortical System," *Sleep Medicine Reviews* (April 2002), 125–138.

p. 68 F. Chang and M. R. Opp, "Corticotropin-Releasing Hormone (CRH) as a Regulator of Waking," *Neuroscience and Biobehavior Reviews* (July 2001), 445–453.

p. 68 Steiger.

p. 69 Díaz-Muñoz et al., "Correlation between Blood Adenosine Metabolism and Sleep in Humans," *Sleep Research Online* (February 1999), 33–41.

p. 69 Tina Hesman, "Fly Naps Inspire Dreams of Sleep Genetics," *Science News* (Feb. 19, 2000), 117.

p. 69 T. Porkka-Heiskanen et al., "Adenosine: A Mediator of the Sleep-Inducing Effects of Prolonged Wakefulness," *Science* (May 23, 1997), 1265–1268.

p. 69 S. Moriarty, D. Rainnie, R. McCarley, and R. Greene, "Disinhibition of Ventrolateral Preoptic Sleep-active Neurons by Adenosine: A New Mechanism for Sleep Promotion," *Neuroscience* (123(2), 2004, month not available), 451–457.

p. 69 J. Travis, "Napless Cats Awaken Interest in Adenosine," *Science News* (May 24, 1997), 316.

p. 70 M. A. Carskadon and W. C. Dement, "Daytime Sleepiness: Quantification of a Behavioral State," *Neuroscience and Biobehavior Reviews* (Fall 1987), 307–317.

p. 71 K. A. Bazar, A. J. Yun, and P. Y. Lee, "Debunking a Myth: Neurohormonal and Vagal Modulation of Sleep Centers, Not Redistribution of Blood Flow, May Account for Postprandial Somnolence," *Medical Hypotheses* (September–October 2004), 778–782.

p. 71 G. K. Zammit, S. H. Ackerman, R. Shindledecker, et al., "Postprandial Sleep and Thermogenesis in Normal Men," *Physiology and Behavior* (August 1992), 251–259.

p. 71 David Schardt, "Perchance to Dream," *Nutrition Action Newsletter* (September 1999).

p. 71 J. M. Siegel, "Sleep," *Encarta*.

p. 74 T. Deboer, S. Overeem, N. A. H. Visser, et al., "Convergence of Circadian and Sleep Regulatory Mechanisms on Hypocretin-1," *Neuroscience* (July 2004), 727–732.

p. 74 C. P. Cannon, C. H. McCabe, P. H. Stone, et al., "Circadian Variation in the Onset of Unstable Angina and Non-Q Wave Acute Myocardial Infarction (The TIMI III Registry and TIMI IIIB)," *American Journal of Cardiology* (February 1, 1997), 253–258.

p. 74 N. N. Jarjour, "Circadian Variation in Allergen and Nonspecific Bronchial Responsiveness in Asthma," *Chronobiology International* (September 1999), 631–639.

p. 75 R. Ben-Shlomo and C. P. Kyriacou, "Circadian Rhythm Entrainment in Flies and Mammals," *Cell Biochemistry and Biophysics* (October 2002), 141–156.

p. 75 S. Panda, M. P. Antoch, B. H. Miller, et al., "Coordinated Transcription of Key Pathways in the Mouse by the Circadian Clock," *Cell* (May 3, 2002), 307–320.

p. 76 Karen Wright, "Times of Our Lives," *Scientific American* (September 2002), 58–65.

p. 76 Quoted in Wright.

p. 76 Michael Hastings, "A Gut Feeling for Time," *Nature* (May 23, 2002), 391–392.

p. 76 M. Y. Cheng, C. M. Bullock, C. Li, et al., "Prokineticin 2 Transmits the Behavioural Circadian Rhythm of the Suprachiasmatic Nucleus," *Nature* (May 23, 2002), 405–410.

p. 77 Wright, 2002.

p. 77 D. M. Berson, F. A. Dunn, and M. Takao, "Phototransduction by Retinal Ganglion Cells That Set the Circadian Clock," *Science* (February 8, 2002), 1070–1073.

p. 77 Michael Menaker, "Circadian Photoreception," Science (January 10, 2003), 213.

p. 78 S. Labyak, "Sleep and Circadian Schedule Disorders," *The Nursing Clinics of North America* (December 2002), 599–610.

p. 78 T. K. Tamai, V. Vardhanabhuti, S. Arthur, et al., "Flies and Fish: Birds of a Feather," *Journal of Neuroendocrinology* (April 2003), 344–349.

p. 79 T. S. Horowitz, B. E. Cade, J. M. Wolfe, and C. A. Czeisler, "Efficacy of Bright Light and

Sleep/Darkness Scheduling in Alleviating Circadian Maladaptation to Night Work," *American Journal of Physiology: Endocrinology and Metabolism* (August 2001), E384–E391.

p. 79 B. H. Karlsson, A. K. Knutsson, B. O. Lindahl, and L. S. Alfredsson, "Metabolic Disturbances in Male Workers with Rotating Three-Shift Work. Results of the WOLF Study," *International Archives of Occupational and Environmental Health* (July 2003), 424–430.

p. 79 Op. cit.

p. 79 L. K. Barger, B. E. Cade, N. T. Ayas, et al., "Extended Work Shifts and the Risk of Motor Vehicle Crashes among Interns," *New England Journal of Medicine* (January 13, 2005), 125–134.

p. 79 S. Garbarino, L. Nobil, M. Beelke, et al., "Sleep Disorders and Daytime Sleepiness in State Police Shiftworkers," *Archives of Environmental Health* (March/April 2002), 167–173.

p. 81 Al Frank, "Injuries Related to Shiftwork," *American Journal of Preventive Medicine* (May 2000 supplement), 33–36.

p. 81 D. H. Bovbjerg, "Circadian Disruption and Cancer: Sleep and Immune Regulation," *Brain, Behavior, and Immunity* (February 15, 2003), S48–S50.

p. 81 S. Garbarino, M. Beelke, G. Costa, et al., "Brain Function and Effects of Shift Work: Implications for Clinical Neuropharmacology," *Neuropsychobiology* (January 2002), 50–56.

p. 81 D. C. Mohren, N. W. Jansen, I. J. Kantu, et al., "Prevalence of Common Infections among Employees in Different Work Schedules," *Journal of Occupational and Environmental Medicine* (November 2002), 1003–1011.

p. 81 Tamai et al., 2003.

p. 81 E. I. Challet, I. Caldelas, C. Graff, and P. Pévet, "Synchronization of the Molecular Clockwork by Light- and Food-Related Cues in Mammals," *Biological Chemistry* (May 2003), 711–719.

p. 81 H. J. Burgess, S. J. Crowley, C. J. Gazda, et al., "Preflight Adjustment to Eastward Travel: 3 Days of Advancing Sleep with and without Morning Bright Light," *Journal of Biological Rhythms* (August 2003), 318–328.

p. 82 R. L. Spitzer, M. Terman, J. B. W. Williams, et al., "Jet Lag: Clinical Features, Validation of a New Syndrome-Specific Scale, and Lack of Response to Melatonin in a Randomized, Double-Blind Trial," *American Journal of Psychiatry* (September 1999), 1392–1396.

p. 82 L. G. Almeida Montes, M. P. Ontiveros Uribe, J. Cortés Sotres, and G. Heinze Martin, "Treatment of Primary Insomnia with Melatonin: A Double-Blind, Placebo-Controlled, Crossover Study," *Journal of Psychiatry & Neuroscience* (May 2003), 191–196.

p. 83 I. V. Zhdanova and V. Tucci, "Melatonin, Circadian Rhythms, and Sleep," *Current Treatment Options in Neurology* (May 1, 2003), 225–229.

p. 83 Ibid.

p. 83 S. Higuchi, Y. Motohashi, Y. Liu, et al., "Effects of VDT Tasks with a Bright Display at Night on Melatonin, Core Temperature, Heart Rate, and Sleepiness," *Journal of Applied Physiology* (May 2003), 1773–1776.

p. 84 C. M. Portas, K. Krakow, P. Allen, et al., "Auditory Processing Across the Sleep-Wake Cycle: Simultaneous EEG and fMRI Monitoring in Humans," *Neuron* (December 2000), 991–999.

p. 85 Robert Stickgold, "Watching the Sleeping Brain Watch Us—Sensory Processing during Sleep," *Trends in Neuroscience* (June 2001), 307–308.

p. 85 M. Cheour, O. Martynova, R. Näätänen, et al., "Psychobiology: Speech Sounds Learned by Sleeping Newborns," *Nature* (February 2, 2002), 599–600.

p. 85 T. J. Sejnowski and A. Destexhe, "Why Do We Sleep?" *Brain Research* (December 15, 2000), 208–223.

p. 86 Personal communication.

p. 86 Marcos G. Frank, Naoum P. Issa, and Michael P. Stryker, "Sleep Enhances Plasticity in the Developing Visual Cortex," *Neuron* (April 2001), 275–287.

p. 86 J. De Koninck, D. Lorrain, G. Christ, et al., "Intensive Language Learning and Increases in REM Sleep: Evidence of a Performance Factor," *International Journal of Psychophysiology* (vol. 8, 1989, month not available), 43–47.

p. 87 P. Maquet, S. Laureys, P. Peigneus et al. , "Experience-dependent Changes in Cerebral Activation During REM Sleep," *Nature Neuroscience* (August 2000), 831–836.

p. 87 R. P. Vertes, "Memory Consolidation in Sleep: Dream or Reality," *Neuron* (September 30, 2004), 135–148.

p. 87 R. P. Vertes and K. E. Eastman, "The Case Against Memory Consolidation in REM Sleep," *Behavioral & Brain Sciences* (2000, special issue), 867–876.

p. 87 M. P. Walker and R. Stickgold, "Sleep-Dependent Learning and Memory Consolidation," *Neuron* (September 30, 2004), 121–133.

p. 87 R. D. Cartwright, "The Role of Sleep in Changing Our Minds: A Psychologist's Discussion of Papers on Memory Reactivation and Consolidation in Sleep," *Learning & Memory* (November–December 2004), 660–663.

p. 88 U. Wagner, S. Gais, H. Haider, et al., "Sleep Inspires Insight," *Nature* (January 22, 2004), 352–354.

p. 88 R. Cartwright, A. Luten, M. Young, et al., "Role of REM Sleep and Dream Affect in Overnight Mood Regulation: A Study of Normal Volunteers," *Psychiatry Research* (October 19, 1998), 1–8.

p. 91 M. Barinaga, "A Time to Rest: Clock Signal Identified," *Science* (December 21, 2001), 2453–2454; A. Kramer, Fu-Chia Yang, P. Snodgrass, et al., "Regulation of Daily Locomotor Activity and Sleep by Hypothalamic FGF Receptor Signaling," *Science* (December 21, 2001), 2511–2515.

p. 92 K. Lee and C. A. Landis, "Priorities for Sleep Research During the Next Decade," *Research in Nursing and Health* (June 2003), 1–2.

p. 93 *2003 National Sleep Disorders Research Plan,* NIH Publication No. 03-5209, (July 2003), vii.

p. 93 Maurice M. Ohayon, "Epidemiology of Insomnia: What We Know and What We Still Need to Learn," *Sleep Medicine Reviews* (May 2002), 97–111.

p. 93 B. Corman and D. Leger, "Sleep Disorders in the Elderly," *Revue du Praticien* (French) (June 30, 2004), 1281–1285.

p. 93 "2002 'Sleep in America' Poll," National Sleep Foundation.

p. 93 V. Wooten, "Medical Causes of Insomnia," in M. H. Kryger, T. Roth, and W. C. Dement (Eds.), *Principles and Practice of Sleep Medicine* (Philadelphia: Saunders, 1994), 509–522.

p. 93 C. H. Bastien, A. Vallieres, and C. M. Morin, "Precipitating Factors of Insomnia," *Behavioral Sleep Medicine* (2[1], 2004, month not available), 50–62.

p. 95 C. M. Morin, C. Colecchi, J. Stone, et al., "Behavioral and Pharmacological Therapies for Late-Life Insomnias: A Randomized Controlled Trial," *Journal of the American Medical Association* (March 17, 1999), 991–999.

p. 95 A. G. Harvey and S. Payne, "The Management of Unwanted Pre-sleep Thoughts in Insomnia: Distraction with Imagery Versus General Distraction," *Behaviour Research and Therapy* (March 2002), 267–277.

p. 96 "2002 'Sleep in America' Poll."

p. 96 E. O. Bixler, A. N. Vgontzas, L. M. Lin, et al., "Association of Hypertension and Sleep-Disordered Breathing," *Archives of Internal Medicine* (August 14, 2000), 2289–2295.

p. 97 Quoted from an interview with reporter Ben Knight, ABC News, December 19, 2003, available on-line at <www.anc.net.au>.

p. 99 P. W. Olejniczak and B. J. Fisch, "Sleep Disorders," *Medical Clinics of North America* (July 2003), 803–833.

p. 99 S. Gilman, R. D. Chervin, R. A. Koeppe, et al., "Obstructive Sleep Apnea is Related to a Thalamic Cholinergic Deficit in MSA," *Neurology* (July 8, 2003), 35–39.

p. 100 F. J. Nieto, T. B. Young, B. K. Lind, et al., "Association of Sleep-Disordered Breathing, Sleep Apnea, and Hypertension in a Large Community-Based Study," *Journal of the American Medical Association* (April 12, 2000), 1829–1836.

p. 100 N. Meslier, F. Gagnadoux, P. Giraud, et al., "Impaired Glucose-Insulin Metabolism in Males with Obstructive Sleep Apnoea Syndrome," *European Respiratory Journal* (July 2003), 156–160.

p. 100 R. Wolk and V. K. Somers, "Cardiovascular Consequences of Obstructive Sleep Apnea," Clinics in Chest Medicine (June 2003), 195–205; H. Yaggi and V. Mohsenin, "Sleep-Disordered Breathing and Stroke," *Clinics in Chest Medicine* (June 2003), 223–237.

p. 100 "Sleep Apnea Impairs Blood Pressure Regulation," press release from the Mayo Clinic, November 21, 2000.

p. 101 L. Findley, C. Smith, J. Hooper, et al., "Treatment with Nasal CPAP Decreases Automobile Accidents in Patients with Sleep Apnea." *American Journal of Respiratory Care Medicine* (March 2000), 857–859.

p. 101 L. E. Krahn, J. L. Black, and M. H. Silber, "Narcolepsy: New Understanding of Irresistible Sleep," *Mayo Clinic Proceedings* (February 2001), 185–194.

p. 102 M. Hungs, J. Fan, L. Lin, et al., "Identification and Functional Analysis of Mutations in the Hypocretin (Orexin) Genes of Narcoleptic Canines," *Genome Research* (April 2001), 531–539.

p. 102 R. E. Brown, "Involvement of Hypocretins/Orexins in Sleep Disorders and Narcolepsy," *Drug News and Perspectives* (April 2003), 1–5.

p. 102 S. Nashino, B. Ripley, S. Overeem, et al., "Hypocretin (Orexin) Deficiency in Human Narcolepsy," *Lancet* (January 1, 2000), 39–40.

p. 102 T. C. Thannickal, R. Y. Moore, R. Nienhuis, et al., "Reduced Number of Hypocretin Neurons in Human Narcolepsy," *Neuron* (September 2000), 469–474.

p. 102 E. Mignot, "Sleep, Sleep Disorders and Hypocretin," *Sleep Medicine* (vol. 5, supp. 1, June 2004), S2–S8.

p. 102 "Narcolepsy More Common in Men, Often Originates in Their 20s," *Science Daily* magazine, Mayo Clinic, available on-line at <www.mayo.edu> (April 29, 2002).

p. 102 J. E. Black, S. N. Brooks, and S. Nishino, "Narcolepsy and Syndromes of Primary Excessive Daytime Somnolence," *Seminars in Neurology* (September 2004), 271–282.

p. 103 National Institutes of Health, National Center on Sleep Disorders Research and Office of Prevention, Education, and Control. *Working Group Report on Problem Sleepiness* (August 1997).

p. 104 D. Barrett and M. Loeffler, "Comparison of Dream Content of Depressed vs. Nondepressed Dreamers." *Psychological Reports* (April 1992), 403–406; R. Armitage, A. Rochlen, T. Fitch, et al., "Dream Recall and Major Depression: A Preliminary Report," *Dreaming* (September 1995), 189–198.

p. 104 Ronald E. Dahl, "The Consequences of Insufficient Sleep for Adolescents: Links Between Sleep and Emotional Regulation," *Phi Delta Kappan* (January 1999), 354–359.

p. 104 U. Rao, R. E. Dahl, N. D. Ryan, et al., "The Relationship Between Longitudinal Clinical Course and Sleep and Cortisol Changes in Adolescent Depression," *Biological Psychiatry* (September 15, 1996), 474–484.

p. 104 Quoted in Judy Foreman, "So, You're Stuck in Sleep-Loss Hell," *The Boston Globe,* July 14, 1997.

p. 105 L. Kayumov, G. Brown, R. Jindal, et al., "A Randomized, Double-Blind, Placebo-Controlled Crossover Study of the Effect of Exogenous Melatonin on Delayed Sleep Phase Syndrome," *Psychosomatic Medicine* (January–February 2001), 40–48.

p. 105 J. K. Wyatt, "Delayed Sleep Phase Syndrome: Pathophysiology and Treatment Options," *Sleep* (September 15, 2004), 1195–1203.

p. 105 K. L. Toh, C. R. Jones, Y. He, et al., "An hPer2 Phosphorylation Site Mutation in Familial Advanced Sleep Phase Syndrome," *Science* (February 9, 2001), 1040–1043.

p. 107 S. Labyak, "Sleep and Circadian Schedule Disorders," *The Nursing Clinics of North America* (December 2002), 599–610.

p. 107 R. D. Chervin, K. H. Archbold, J. E. Dillon, et al., "Associations between Symptoms of Inattention, Hyperactivity, Restless Legs, and Periodic Leg Movements," *Sleep* (March 15, 2002), 213–218.

p. 107 C. M. Bestue, F. X. Sanmarti, and S. J. Artigas, "Periodic Movements of the Limbs During Sleep in Childhood," *Review of Neurology* (February 1–15, 2002), 244–248.

p. 109 S. S. Rajaram, A. S. Walters, S. J. England, et al., "Some Children with Growing Pains May Actually Have Restless Legs Syndrome," *Sleep* (June 15, 2004), 767–773.

p. 109 Matthew M. Clark, "Restless Legs Syndrome," *Journal of the American Board of Family Practice* (September 2001), 368–374.

p. 109 J. Winkelmann, B. Muller-Myhsok, H. U. Wittchen, et al., "Complex Segregation Analysis of Restless Legs Syndrome Provides Evidence for an Autosomal Dominant Mode of Inheritance in Early Age Onset Families," *Annals of Neurology* (September 2002), 297–302.

p. 109 S. Lesage and C. J. Hurley, "Restless Legs Syndrome," *Current Treatment Options in Neurology* (May 2004), 209–219.

p. 109 "Cause for Restless Legs Syndrome," press release from Pennsylvania State University College of Medicine, June 10, 2003.

p. 110 The Johns Hopkins Center for Restless Legs Syndrome at <http://www.neuro.jhmi.edu/rls/treatment.htm>.

p. 110 Quoted in "Melatonin Helps Alleviate Violent Sleep Disorder Symptoms," press release from the Mayo Clinic, September 8, 2003.

p. 110 S. Gilman, R. A. Koeppe, R. D. Chervin, et al., "REM Sleep Behavior Disorder Is Related to Striatal Monoaminergic Deficit in MSA," *Neurology* (July 8, 2003), 29–34.

p. 110 K. Stiasny-Kolster, Y. Doerr, J. C. Möller, et al., "Combination of 'Idiopathic' REM Sleep Behaviour Disorder and Olfactory Dysfunction as Possible Indicator for α-synucleinopathy Demonstrated by Dopamine Transporter FP-CIT-SPECT," *Brain* (January 2005), 126–137.

p. 111 B. F. Boeve, M. H. Silber, and T. J. Ferman, "Melatonin for Treatment of REM Sleep Behavior Disorder in Neurologic Disorders: Results in 14 Patients," *Sleep Medicine* (July 2003), 281–284.

p. 111 "In the Dead of the Night," *The Observer* (United Kingdom), November 18, 2001.

p. 111 "Alien Abductions Diagnosed as a Bad Night's Sleep," *Current Science* (November 17, 2000), page numbers not available.

p. 114 *Marijuana Research Findings: 1980,* National Institute of Drug Abuse Research Monograph

Series, Number 31, U.S. Department of Health and Human Services, Publication Number 80-1001, p. 68.

p. 115 R. D. Peters, E. Kloeppel. E. Alicandri, et al., "Effects of Partial and Total Sleep Deprivation on Driving Performance," Federal Highway Administration Publication No. FHWA-RD-94-046.

p. 115 National Highway Traffic Safety Administration, National Heart, Lung, and Blood Institute, and the National Center on Sleep Disorders Research, *Drowsy Driving and Automobile Crashes: Report and Recommendations,* DOT HS 808 707 (April 1998), 1.

p. 115 National Sleep Foundation, "Adolescent Sleep Needs and Patterns."

p. 115 C. Holden, "Wake-up Call for Sleep Research," *Science* (January 15, 1993), 305.

p. 116 A. M. Williamson and A. M. Feyer, "Moderate Sleep Deprivation Produces Impairments in Cognitive and Motor Performance Equivalent to Legally Prescribed Levels of Alcohol Intoxication," *Occupational and Environmental Medicine* (October 2000), 649–655.

p. 116 Judith Owens, J. Todd Arnedt, et al., "Sleep Loss and Driving Do Not Mix for Medical Residents," presented at the 2003 meeting of Pediatric Academic Societies, April 25, 2003.

p. 117 D. Dawson and K. Reid, "Fatigue, Alcohol, and Performance Impairment," *Nature* (July 17, 1997), 235.

p. 117 Quoted in "Sleep Loss and Driving Do Not Mix for Medical Residents, Study Finds," press release from Brown University, May 3, 2003.

p. 118 J. Connor, R. Norton, S. Ameratunga, et al., "Driver Sleepiness and Risk of Serious Injury to Car Occupants: Population Based Case Control Study," *British Medical Journal* (May 11, 2002), 1125.

p. 118 NSF Statement Regarding Maggie's Law—"Nation's First Law Aimed at Drowsy Driving," National Sleep Foundation, at <http://www.sleepfoundation.org/Press Archives/maggiestmnt.cfm>.

p. 119 S. J. O'Meara, "Eyes Wide Open: The Sleepwalkers," *Odyssey* (January 2002), 32–34.

p. 119 Quoted in O'Meara.

p. 119 "Adult Sleepwalking May Be a Genetic Disorder," press release from the American Academy of Neurology, April 5, 2002.

p. 119 A. Remulla and C. Guilleminault, "Somnambulism (Sleepwalking)," *Expert Opinion on Pharmacotherapy* (October 2004), 2069–2074.

p. 120 W. H. Moorcroft, *Understanding Sleep and Dreaming* (New York: Plenum, 2003), 228–229.

p. 120 Moorcroft, p. 229.

p. 122 A. Rechtschaffen and B. M. Bergmann, "Sleep Deprivation in the Rat by the Disk-Over-Water Method," *Behavioural Brain Research* (July–August 1995), 55–63.

p. 122 M. M. Eiland, L. Ramanathan, S. Gulyani, et al., "Increases In Amino-Cupric-Silver Staining of the Supraoptic Nucleus after Sleep Deprivation," *Brain Research* (July 26, 2002), 1–8.

p. 123 D. G. Sundstrom and H. M. Dreher, "A Deadly Prion Disease: Fatal Familial Insomnia," *Journal of Neuroscience Nursing* (December 2003), 300–305.

p. 123 S. Coren, *Sleep Thieves: An Eye-opening Exploration into the Science and Mysteries of Sleep* (New York: Free Press Paperbacks, 1996), 11.

p. 127 "2002 'Sleep in America' Poll," p. 9.

p. 128 "Discover Dialogue: Freud-Debunker Bill Domhoff: Dream Un-weaver," *Discover* (March 2002), 16.

p. 129 J. F. Pagel, "Nightmares and Disorders of Dreaming," *American Family Physician* (April 1, 2000), 2037–2042ff.

p. 129 Table adapted from D. Kahn, E. F. Pace-Schott, and J. A. Hobson, "Consciousness in Waking and Dreaming: The Roles of Neuronal Oscillation and Neuromodulation in Determining Similarities and Differences," *Neuroscience* (February 27, 1997), 13–38.

p. 130 November 3, 2003 issue, p. 122.

p. 130 NAPS E-mail alert, March 25, 2002.

p. 130 A. L. Zadra, T. A. Nielsen, and D. C. Donder, "Prevalence of Auditory, Olfactory, and Gustatory Experiences in Home Dreams," *Perceptual and Motor Skills* (December 1998), 819–826.

p. 132 G. W. Domhoff, "A New Neurocognitive Theory of Dreams," *Dreaming* (March 2001), 13–33.

p. 132 Pagel, 2000.

p. 132 D. Picchioni, B. Goeltzenleucher, D. N. Green, et al., "Nightmares as a Coping Mechanism for Stress," *Dreaming* (September 2002), 155–159.

p. 133 P. Lavie, "Posttraumatic Nightmares," in M. A. Carskadon (Ed.), *Encyclopedia of Sleep and Dreaming* (New York: Macmillan, 1993), 464–465.

p. 133 Pagel, 2000.

p. 133 University of Michigan Health System, "Nightmares," available on-line at <http://www.med .umich.edu/1libr/pa/pa_bnitemar_hhg.htm>.

p. 133 Pagel, 2000.

p. 134 A. L. Zadra and T. A. Nielsen, "Topographical EEG Mapping in a Case of Recurrent Sleep Terrors," *Dreaming* (June 1998), 67–74.

p. 135 Debra A. Titone, "Memories Bound: The Neuroscience of Dreams," *Trends in Cognitive Sciences* (January 2002), 4–5.

p. 136 "Dreams May Provide Glimpse into Subconscious of Divorced Depressed Patients," press release from Rush Presbyterian St. Luke's Medical Center, January 2002.

p. 137 J. Kroth, A. Daline, D. Longstreet, et al., "Sleep, Dreams, and Job Satisfaction," *Psychological Reports* (June 2002), 876–878.

p. 138 J. Kroth, L. Thompson, J. Jackson et al., "Dream Characteristics of Stock Brokers after a Major Market Downturn," *Psychological Reports* (June 2002), 1097–1100.

p. 138 G. William Domhoff, "The Purpose of Dreams," available on-line at <http://psych.ucsc.edu /dreams/Articles/purpose.html>.

p. 139 M. J. Fosse, R. Fosse, A. Hobson, and R. J. Stickgold, "Dreaming and Episodic Memory: A Functional Dissociation?" *Journal of Cognitive Neuroscience* (January 2003), 1–9.

p. 139 J. M. Lowenstein, "Such Stuff as Dreams Are Made On," *California Wild (The Magazine of the California Academy of Sciences)* (Summer 1997), 46–48.

p. 139 Domhoff, "The Purpose of Dreams."

p. 140 Estimates from the National Sleep Foundation.

p. 140 David Foulkes, *Children's Dreaming and the Development of Consciousness* (Cambridge, MA: Harvard University Press, 1999).

p. 141 J. J. Pagel, "Non-dreamers," *Sleep Medicine* (May 2003), 235–241.

p. 141 C. S. Hall, G. W. Domhoff, K. A. Blick, and K. E. Weesner, "The Dreams of College Men and Women in 1950 and 1980: A Comparison of Dream Contents and Sex Differences," *Sleep* (5[2], 1982), 188–194.

p. 142 G. W. Domhoff, *The Scientific Study of Dreams: Neural Networks, Cognitive Development, and Content Analysis* (Washington, DC: American Psychological Association, 2003).

p. 142 Source cited as Dreaming Journal in B. Kantrowitz and K. Springen, "What Dreams Are Made Of," *Newsweek* (August 9, 2004), 42.

p. 143 "Discover Dialogue."

p. 143 Adapted from Moorcroft, 139–140.

p. 144 I. Raymond, T. A. Nielsen, G. Lavigne, and M. Choinier, "Incorporation of Pain in Dreams of Hospitalized Burn Victims," *Sleep* (November 1, 2002), 765–770.

p. 144 D. M. Wegner, R. M. Wenzlaff, and M. Kozak, "Dream Rebound: The Return of Suppressed Thoughts in Dreams," *Psychological Science* (April 2004), 232–236.

p. 144 T. A. Nielsen, "Changes in the Kinesthetic Content of Dreams Following Somatosensory Stimulation of Leg Muscles during REM Sleep," *Dreaming* (June 1993), 99–113.

p. 144 R. Cartwright and I. Romanek, "Repetitive Dreams of Normal Subjects," *Sleep Research* (vol. 7, 1978, month not available), 174.

p. 145 S. LaBerge, "Lucid Dreaming: Psychophysiological Studies of Consciousness during REM Sleep," in R. R. Bootzen, et al., (Eds.), *Sleep and Cognition* (Washington, DC: American Psychological Association, 1990), 109–126.

p. 145 A. Damasio, *The Feeling of What Happens* (New York: Harcourt Brace, 1999).

p. 145 P. D. Tyson, R.D. Ogilvie, and H. T. Hunt, "Lucid, Prelucid, and Nonlucid Dreams Related to the Amount of EEG Alpha Activity during REM Sleep," *Psychophysiology* (July 1984), 442–451.

p. 145 L. da Silva, "Visual Dreams in the Congenitally Blind?" *Trends in Cognitive Science* (August 2003), 328–330.

p. 146 C. S. Hall, "A Ubiquitous Sex Difference in Dreams Revisited," *Journal of Personality and Social Psychology* (May 1984), 1109–1117.

p. 146 D. Foulkes and S. Fleisher, "Mental Activity in Relaxed Wakefulness," *Journal of Abnormal Psychology* (February 1975), 66–75.

p. 147 Personal communication.

p. 147 Personal communication.

p. 148 M. Jouvet, *The Paradox of Sleep: The Study of Dreaming* (Cambridge, MA: MIT Press, 2001).

p. 149 D. Halber, "Animals Have Complex Dreams," press release from the Massachusetts Institute of Technology, January 31, 2001.

p. 149 Personal communication.

INDEX

Page numbers in *italics* refer to illustrations.